Remember Me

Remember Me

The Charles Morgan Blessing Story

Mervyn Dykes

hancock

house

ISBN 978-0-88839-627-3
Copyright © 2010 Mervyn Dykes

Cataloging in Publication Data

Dykes, Mervyn
    Remember me : the Charles Morgan Blessing story
    / Mervyn Dykes.

    Includes index.
    Also available in electronic format.
    ISBN 978-0-88839-627-3

    1. Blessing, Charles Morgan. 2. Murder—British Columbia
— Cariboo (Regional district). 3. Cariboo (B.C. : Regional
district) — Gold discoveries. 4. Gold miners — British Columbia
— Cariboo (Regional district) — Biography. I. Title.

HV6535.C33B36 2009   364.152'30971175   C2009-903851-X

Printed in South Korea — PACOM

Editor: Theresa Laviolette
Production: Mia Hancock
Cover Design: Ingird Luters
Photographs courtesy Hancock House archives unless otherwise indicated.
Front and back cover images: Mervyn Dykes

*We acknowledge the financial support of the Government of Canada through the
Book Publishing Industry Development Program (BPIDP) for our publishing activities.*

Published simultaneously in Canada and the United States by

HANCOCK HOUSE PUBLISHERS LTD.
19313 Zero Avenue, Surrey, B.C. Canada V3S 9R9
(604) 538-1114 Fax (604) 538-2262

HANCOCK HOUSE PUBLISHERS
1431 Harrison Avenue, Blaine, WA U.S.A. 98230-5005
(604) 538-1114 Fax (604) 538-2262

Website: www.hancockhouse.com
Email: sales@hancockhouse.com

Contents

Prologue

There are places in the Cariboo where, if you wander a few steps off the trail, you can travel back in time for hundreds of years. Charles Morgan Blessing sleeps in one of these places. His friends laid the young prospector to rest there back in 1866 and he dreams on still.

Like thousands of other young men, Charlie heeded the call to go west to make his fortune. He first dipped his gold pan in the rivers and streams of California and then headed north to newer strikes in British Territory. He was in a hurry to join up with friends prospecting near a shantytown named Van Winkle and that haste, coupled with two classic mistakes, was to cost him his life. Now, his gravesite with its weathered wooden headboard has become the smallest provincial historic park in British Columbia, the western-most province of Canada.

Like countless prospectors and tourists before me, I have taken the old Gold Rush Trail north from New Westminster on the banks of the Fraser River in British Columbia. I have traveled the road between Quesnel and the golden gravel of Williams Creek. I have stopped beside the roadside marker that points the way to Charlie's grave. I have taken those few steps into the bush that turn back time. I have felt the spirit of the lonely, tree-clad slope where the body is now interred.

When I first stood there at the foot of the grave, flailing away at mosquitoes, the prevailing impression was one of bewilderment. Not mine, but, I fancy, some echo from Charlie's last mortal moments. When I close my eyes I can almost see him sitting there, naive, trusting, with his back turned to his killer. I sense his astonishment in that instant when the shot boomed out and he teetered on the cusp of two worlds. This good, gentle man had set out for the Cariboo with dreams of gold, but had found death instead.

If all this sounds melodramatic, please excuse me. I can't help it, because Charlie Blessing pushed his way into my life and practically demanded that I tell his story. This has never happened to me before and, as with all unusual experiences, it is difficult to describe accurately. Let us make a start though, and see what happens.

Folklore has it that if you spend more than two weeks at Barkerville on Williams Creek and have any imagination at all, you are doomed to be drawn back forever. That's what happened to me. There is something about the town that gets under your skin and never lets you go.

I first visited Barkerville in the winter of 1987 to write a magazine article, and it snatched my heart in seconds. As I walked enchanted through knee-deep snow in street shoes and business suit, I vowed to bring my family back in the summer when the former gold rush town enjoys its new life as a provincial historical site.

During this second visit, I walked into the office of *The Sentinel* and watched a volunteer printing reproductions of the pioneer newspaper.

As I scanned my copy, a small news item on the front page jumped out at me. It was headed "Body Found on Trail" and said the dead man was believed to be a missing prospector named Charles Morgan Blessing. Something about the name intrigued me, and as I stuffed the newspaper in my camera bag I vowed to find out more about him.

My researches were spread over many years between other projects. And of course there was a third visit to Barkerville…and a fourth…We even made enquiries about property in nearby Wells, a 1930s gold rush town. I took photographs of locations important to Charlie's story. I spent many hours in libraries and the Provincial Archives in Victoria. I went bug-eyed reading microfilmed copies of *The Sentinel.* I learned how to pan for gold and started a rock collection. I read the bench notes Judge Matthew Baillie Begbie made during the trial of Charlie's killer. And I pored through scores of accounts of life in this part of the world during the latter half of the nineteenth century.

I soon discovered that the story of Blessing's murder contains all the drama of a Hollywood Western. There's the classic good guy–bad guy thing, the loyal sidekick, saloons, dance hall gals, a gold rush, a shooting, the stirring pursuit of a villain, a trial by a feisty judge, and eventually a hanging. However, there are two big problems along the way.

Firstly, most of the accounts I read appeared to have been preserved orally and written down by others much later. This laid them open to distortion by suspect memories and embellishment as each teller of the tale attempted to improve on what had been told before. "I know someone who knew so-and-so who told him…" The stories produced in this fashion are often riddled with errors and contradictions. In some cases even the names of the principals are incorrect. A few of these mistakes have been perpetuated by later writers and upgraded to the status of "facts." Some of the end product is now lurid enough to grace not only the pages of the dime novels of Charlie's day, but the supermarket tabloids of our own time.

Secondly, the rarity of contemporary reports of Charlie's background and death is only part of the problem. Some of the first-hand accounts have huge holes in them that ask more questions than they answer. You can fill these holes in two ways: by research, or by making up stuff. Sometimes the cautious storyteller might try to cover himself by saying, "This is only my opinion, but…" Chances are that when one of the listeners repeats the tale, the qualifier will be lost and everything will be treated as fact.

The effect of all this has been to distance Charlie from reality and move him closer to the world of legend. Unless something is done soon, he will vanish into myth like Robin Hood and King Arthur and no one will be able to separate truth from fiction any more.

Perhaps Charlie sensed that this would happen. Just before he left Quesnellemouth, as Quesnel was then called, he urged a friend not to forget him.

"My name is Charles Morgan Blessing," he said. "Be sure to recollect it if anything should happen to me in this country."

Charlie wanted to be remembered, but on his own terms.

My own search for the truth about Charles Morgan Blessing eventually took me to Judge Begbie's bench notes and *The Sentinel's* accounts of the trial. I decided to make these my core material and discard whatever didn't measure up against them.

In my time as a journalist I have spent many years covering the various types of court. I soon learned that the gathering, presentation and recording of evidence is far from being a perfect process. However, in the case of Charles Morgan Blessing it is simply the best there is to work with.

Mervyn Dykes
New Zealand
September 2009

What the Better-dressed Prospectors Wore

While the more affluent gold-seekers were able to pay to have their gear freighted north, others pushed handcarts or even carried their belongings on their backs.

To help them decide what to pack and what to leave out, lists were published in newspapers and distributed. Here is one dating to the 1860s (the values are expressed in the pounds, shillings and pence of the day):

Single Men

Beaverteen jacket 6s/6d
Beaverteen waistcoat with sleeves. . . 4s/4d
Beaverteen trousers, warm-lined 6s/6d
Duck trousers 2s/3d
Coloured drill jacket 2s/9d
Coloured drill trousers 2s/6d
Coloured drill waistcoat. 2s
Pilot overcoat or jacket 10s
    or waterproof coat. 7s/6d
Two blue serge shirts 4s/6d
Felt hat 2s
Brazil straw hat 10d
Six striped, cotton shirts each @ 1s/6d
Pair of boots 8s/6d
Pair of shoes 5s
Four handkerchiefs, each @ 6d
Fours pairs worsted hose each @ . . . 1s
Two pairs cotton hose each @ 9d
Braces. 3d
Four towels each @ 4d
Razor, shaving brush and glass 4s/6d

Single Women

Warm cloak with cape 6s
Two bonnets each @ 3s/10d
Small shawl 2s/3d
Stuff dress 11s
Two print dresses each @ 6s
Two flannel petticoats each @ 2s/6d
Stuff petticoat. 3s/9
Two twill cotton petticoats each @ . . . 2s
Stays 2s/6d
Three capes each @ 10d
Four pocket handkerchiefs each @ . . . 3d
Two net handkerchiefs each @ 5d
Four nightcaps each @ 7d
Four jackets each @ 1s/4d
Two pairs black worsted hose each @ 10d
Four pairs cotton hose each @ 10d
Pair shoes 2s/9d
Pair boots 5s
Six towels each @ 4d

Chapter One

Date With Death

Three people are central to this story — the victim, the killer and the star witness. They were in turn, Charles Morgan Blessing, who is described in contemporary records as a mild-mannered American prospector on his second visit to the Cariboo goldfields; James Barry, billed as a Texas gambler of Irish descent; and Wellington Delaney Moses, an English-born black barber and inveterate journal keeper. Blessing was murdered, Barry was hanged and Moses' diaries became one of the most important sources of information about daily life in the gold rush town of Barkerville.

Their story opens in the spring of 1866 — a time when the border with the Territory of Washington to the south was blurry at best. The British Territory in the northwest was not yet part of the Confederation of Canada and there were fears that the discovery of gold would prompt a takeover by the Americans.

The building of the Cariboo Wagon Road (started 1862 and completed 1865) was much more than a service to miners and traders; it was a political move to strengthen the British grip on the region. The positioning of New Westminster on the hilly northern banks of the Fraser River a few years earlier was no accident either. Any invaders from the south would find themselves faced by a huge "moat" and an uphill fight to take the town.

Long before gold was discovered, riches were already pouring out of the region in the form of furs and salmon. This revenue stream was controlled by the Hudson's Bay Company, which, operating from a network of forts and trading posts, was prepared to defend its monopoly vigorously. A gold strike, with its destabilizing effects, was the last thing the company's officials wanted.

Who was first to find the gold? No one really knows. Some researchers point to a strike by Scottish seaman James Houston at Tranquille Creek in 1857, but others say the native population had known about the gold for years. Whatever the truth, it is clear that for several months at least Hudson's Bay officials traded quietly with Indians and others for gold nuggets and flakes from the Fraser River. They had no choice. If they refused to accept the gold, it would be taken elsewhere and the news would get out in a less-controlled fashion. So they downplayed reports of gold discoveries, placed them in a figurative kettle and jammed the lid down tight.

Early in 1858, the lid blew off.

With the Californian goldfields waning, thousands of restless men were free to respond to whispers of great riches to the north, and the source of the loudest of those whispers was the Hudson's Bay Company itself. By February, the company's store of gold had reached 800 ounces and something had to be done to turn this considerable asset into cash. The gold was slipped aboard the steamer *Otter,* bound for the nearest mint in San Francisco. In that gold-hungry town, the news proved impossible to suppress. Within days, a small, aggressive band of prospectors was heading north, prepared to bull their way past the Hudson's Bay Company and on to the Fraser River.

The paddlewheel steamer *Commodore* reached Fort Victoria on Vancouver Island by April 25, 1858, with 450 men aboard, 60 of whom were British. The bulk of the rest were Americans, Germans, and Italians. At that time the entire population of the southern part of the island was only 400.

Off on their great adventure. A group of miners takes time out to record the moment. Some would find gold at the end of their journey, but others found hardship, disappointed, or even death.

This trickle preceded a flood. That summer alone, more than 30,000 hopeful prospectors steamed north from San Francisco. The gold seekers surged ashore and commandeered anything that would float (and a few things that didn't) to try the often-stormy passage to the mainland. They traveled up the Fraser River to New Westminster and from there were able to board one of the paddle wheelers that churned as far as Yale in the lower reaches of the Fraser Canyon.

James Moore, a member of one of the first parties to arrive, later described how they made history:

> The next morning we left [Fort] Hope and camped on a bar at noon to cook lunch. While doing so, one of our party noticed particles of gold in the moss that was growing on the rocks. On the bar he washed a pan of that moss and got a prospect. After lunch we all prospected and found good pay dirt. We named the bar 'Hill's' after the man who got the first prospect.

Hill's Bar alone was ultimately to yield $2 million but, long before

The scene that greeted travellers at Yale after the riverboat ride from New Westminster around the time that Moses and Blessing travelled together.

then, word of the find was roaring about San Francisco, and the rush was on in earnest.

Those who were first to follow Moore and his companions literally tripped over gold embedded in the sand and gravel of the river bars. One miner wrote home to say:

> We found gold everywhere and my only surprise was that a region so auriferous should have remained so long unproclaimed and hidden from the gaze of civilisation. I found a very choice quartz specimen, six ounces in weight, which contained at least four ounces of gold, half jutting out of the sand on the river's bank. During this day's work seven nuggets, varying from about half an ounce to five ounces in weight were picked up, while the average yield of dust was no less than four ounces each man, and all I had to work with was a gold pan.

One by one the river bars were tested and relieved of a fortune in gold, mostly in the form of small nuggets and fine grains. But with so many men crammed into a relatively small area, there were tensions and disappointments aplenty. Local Indians resented the invasion and several battles were fought. At one time a full-scale war seemed likely between Indians and Americans on British Territory.

The unlucky prospectors and latecomers dismissed the Fraser River strike as humbug, but to the veterans of the Californian fields the message was clear. Most of the gold taken had been small nuggets and "fines" washed and tumbled down the river. Coarser gold and the true mother lode surely lay further north beyond the canyon.

Their first barrier north of Yale was Hell's Gate, where a sudden narrowing of the canyon walls turned the river into a raging torrent and marked the end of the line for the paddle wheelers. Until the Cariboo Wagon Road was blasted through the canyon, the only alternatives were to cling like flies to a stomach-churning network of planks and ropes that Indians had strung high on the cliffs, or else try to detour around the canyon altogether.

Enduring incredible hardships, the adventurers panned and probed their way another 400 miles into the wilderness. Good finds were made at several points, but always before them was the lure of something bigger and better. At what is now known as Williams Creek in the northern Cariboo country they found it, one of the richest gold fields the world has ever known.

Van Winkle is No More

Charles Morgan Blessing was heading for the town of Van Winkle, which, in the late 1860s, was to be found near the creek of the same name some fifteen miles from Barkerville. The town began in 1863 and boomed while the gold lasted.

At one point it had twenty-five businesses established, but only two or three years later had begun to decline. Against the predictions of many, it was still going as late as 1890, but faded away soon after.

The town of Stanley, two miles away to the west, was another boom-and-bust town of which no trace remains today. At one point the two towns had a combined population of between 3,000 and 4,000 people.

Both were close to the gold-rich Lightning Creek and strikes were also made on its tributary, Van Winkle Creek. Somewhere in this area, Charlie's friends were working, but, so far as can be determined, they were never identified and did not come forward when his death was reported.

In the Cariboo, a mountainous region near the center of British Columbia, almost every one of the myriad streams and rills had a fortune to offer. Settlements sprang up around the hot spots, and rose and fell in prominence almost overnight. Barkerville, on Williams Creek, was soon being billed as the biggest city west of Chicago and north of San Francisco.

Among those drawn into this riotous, roaring environment in the spring of 1866 was Charlie Blessing. He was hoping to rejoin friends he had made during his first visit to the Cariboo in 1862. This time, like so many others, he came north by steamer and made his way to New Westminster. There he met Wellington Delaney Moses and the unlikely pair struck up a close friendship.

Blessing's origins are obscure. He has been described variously as coming from a well-to-do Boston family, as being a native of Ohio, and as having lived in "several of the eastern states." He is also said to have operated a successful claim in Calaveras County, California, that set him up for life, but when Moses met him he was wearing clothes that, while of good cut, were no longer new.

Blessing was thirty years old and stood about five feet, ten inches tall. Moses later described him as being shy, almost timid, and "a very moral man." He had light brown hair, rather thin on the crown, and there was usually sparse blonde stubble on his chin and jowls. He smiled often, and sometimes his grin revealed the flash of gold-filled teeth fairly well back in his mouth.

A 1905 report claimed that Moses was an escaped slave from the American South, and had him talking a "yes Massa, no Massa" form of English. That is pure rubbish. Moses was born in London, England in 1815 and was named Wellington in honor of the duke who had just triumphed over Napoleon. While in San Francisco in 1858, he was one of three black men charged with interviewing Governor James Douglas to see if there was a place in the British Territory where others of his race could settle.

Their reception was favorable and they chose Saltspring, one of the smaller islands between Vancouver Island and the mainland. The settlement flourished, but Moses remained in Victoria where, for a short while, he operated the Pioneer Shaving Saloon and Bathroom, which had a private entrance for ladies. He also sold a "hair invigorator" of his own concoction that he claimed would cure scurf and dandruff and, with regular use, even prevent baldness. His marriage failed around this time, and in 1862 he decided to follow the rush to the Cariboo. There he worked as a barber, sold his hair invigorator, made a few loans on the side, and supplied ladies with dresses, ribbons, laces, perfumes, and other knick knacks.

When Blessing met him, Moses had been wintering-over in Victoria, like many of the prospectors. The pair struck up an easy friendship as they traveled by riverboat to Yale, where they parted company. Moses was in no hurry, but Blessing even then was anxious to rejoin his friends whose claim was on Last Chance Creek near Van Winkle, some fifteen miles from Barkerville.

Driven by the impatience that would soon cost him his life, Blessing set off on foot from Yale. Then, perhaps prompted by friendship, or even the near timidity Moses had observed, he stopped. When Moses followed a day or so later, he was surprised to find Blessing waiting for him. The two resumed their travels together and left the town of Junction (now Clinton) at 2:30 p.m. on May 22, 1866. Six days later, at around 7:00 p.m., they reached Quesnellemouth. They had ridden the paddle wheeler *Enterprise*[1] from Soda Creek. Other versions of the tale have them riding north from Yale by stagecoach, but court evidence and Judge Begbie's notes favor the *Enterprise* version.

The two men checked into Brown and Gillis' Occidental Hotel along with other travelers preparing for the final fifty-five-mile slog eastward to Williams Creek. The early part of the next day was spent resting and at one point they were in the hotel bar discussing when to move out. Once again, Blessing was all for leaving immediately. Moses wanted to stay and track down a man who owed him $10 from the previous season.

Neither of them noticed the stocky and somewhat down-at-heel man observing them from close by until he came over and introduced himself as James Barry.[2] Moses said later that he had never seen Barry before, but was startled when the gambler addressed him by name. From this we can assume that he had either made enquiries about the pair, or else had simply been eavesdropping.

As this circa 1890 image shows, many years after Blessing and Moses passed through on their way to the goldfields Quesnellemouth still had the look of a frontier town.

Police records show that earlier Barry had been trying to borrow money from others in the bar. They describe the Texan as being stout rather than stocky, five feet six and a half inches tall and give his age as twenty-nine. His hair and eyes were brown and the hair on his face was said to be "sandy and scant."

"I'll be heading out to the Creek in the morning," Barry told Moses. "Your friend could travel with me."

Moses and Blessing looked at each other uncertainly. There was something about Barry's manner that made them both uneasy. Essentially polite men, they continued an awkward conversation with Barry without making a commitment. At the first opportunity, Blessing leaned close to Moses and whispered that he didn't like the idea of traveling with the stranger.

"Then wait and come with me."

"All right."

Moses considered the matter resolved and went about his own business. Later though, Blessing sought him out with a request that seemed merely odd at the time, but would subsequently assume an awful significance.

"He told me distinctly not to forget his name," Moses testified in court. "He said that it was a singular name and if anything happened to him I would know who it was." Moses had no way of knowing then that Blessing was about to make two classic mistakes, and had less than forty-eight hours to live.

That afternoon, he saw Blessing and Barry sitting on a bench outside the hotel, deep in conversation. Soon after, Blessing told him he had decided to go with Barry after all and that he would be only a day ahead of Moses at Van Winkle. If his friends had no work for him, he would wait there until Moses passed through and go on to Williams Creek with him.

Moses protested. "I don't like that man, Charlie. Why are you going with him?"

"Because I don't want to go broke in the country."

"Charlie," Moses chided, "I haven't got much myself, but you know I'd never see you want." But Blessing's mind was made up. He would go with Barry. That was mistake number one.

The same evening, between seven and eight o'clock, Charlie collected his blankets and gear from their room and went to the bar to settle his bill. The fact that the two friends had chosen to take a room, rather than doss down on the common room floor with other travelers, is an indication that they still had enough money to spare for comforts.

Sometime later, Moses saw Blessing and Barry together in the bar. When Charlie called him over to join them for a farewell drink, Moses went, but he was still full of misgivings. The drinks were ordered and paid for by Blessing.

"He had a rough, coarse shirt on as well as I can recollect," said Moses, "and putting his hand into the breast pocket took out a pocketbook containing money. He took out a twenty-dollar Bank of British Columbia note and I said: 'Charlie you are not broke yet.' He said: 'No, I have a few more of these left.' The barkeeper gave him the change which he placed in a small clasp purse and put in the pocket of his pants." Flashing his roll in a rough bar — that was mistake number two.

Blessing and Barry wanted to make an early start the next day, so, not long after this, they left for an empty house where they planned to spend the night. Moses watched them go uneasily. His nervousness was such that the next morning, May 30, he arose around 5:00 a.m. and went to the house to see if Barry and Blessing had left. They had. He would never see Charlie alive again.

Nothing is known about Moses' own journey to Van Winkle, but we have his word that he reached the town on June 1 and immediately asked around to see if any messages had been left for him. There were none — and no one had seen his friend.

"I arrived at Williams Creek [Barkerville] on June 2 around 10:00 a.m.," he said. "I'm not sure whether it was the following day or a few days later that Barry came into Dixon's shop where I was staying, but I asked him: 'What did you do with my Chummy?'"

"Your Chummy?" Barry replied. "Who's he?"

"The man you left Quesnellemouth with."

"Oh, that coon! I haven't seen him since the morning we left the 'Mouth. I left him on the road. He had a sore foot and couldn't travel."

"Sore foot!" thought Moses. "He's telling me that the man who traveled all the way up here with me gave up because of a sore foot?"

But Barry stared him down, and Moses couldn't think of anything more to say.

During the next few weeks, Moses saw Barry around town several times and asked him on each occasion for news of Blessing. Eventually Barry became angry — Moses said, "savage with me" — and delivered the almost biblical response: "What am I, his keeper?"

Moses couldn't help noticing that the once shabby Barry was now quite well dressed and showed evidence of having money.

Both men observed an uneasy truce for the next few weeks, but Moses thought that if Blessing was still "on the Creek" he would have heard from him one way or another.

Once he had set up shop, old and new customers sought him out; Moses was soon doing brisk business. This gave him plenty of opportunities to ask travelers if they had seen his friend. No one had.

Barry's less down-at-heel appearance was disconcerting, but gamblers often came into money overnight. Similarly, hundreds of the men who trekked to the Cariboo fields had done just what Barry said Blessing had done — given up and gone home. Hundreds more were toiling away on remote creeks, too busy seeking their fortunes to hunt out someone to carry messages to friends.

Consider this hurried letter written by William Cunningham on May 18, 1862:

> Dear Joe, I am well and so are all the rest of the boys. I avail myself of the present opportunity to write you half a dozen lines to let you know that I am well and doing well — making from TWO TO THREE THOUSAND DOLLARS A DAY! Times good — grub high — whisky bad — money plenty. Yours truly, Wm Cunningham.

Even so, Moses continued to worry about his friend as nearly four months went by without word, until September 25 when a man named Joseph Guichon tossed a rock at his supper on the trail near

Joseph Guichon

Joseph Guichon was in charge of a local pack train, which must have been fairly small as there is no mention of anyone helping him. In contrast, a train bringing supplies to the Cariboo from further south usually averaged thirty to fifty mules with two men in the crew for every fifteen or so, and another riding a "bell" mare in the lead. The mules in the train were trained to follow the sound of the bell in the leader's harness. During my researches I met one of Guichon's great grandchildren who said she had been told he was a robust, gruff-spoken, but kindly man.

Guichon worked for one of the most colorful personalities in the Cariboo, John Jacques Caux, who was widely known as Cataline. Caux, or Cataline, hailed from the mountainous Bearn region of France, just over the Pyrenees from Spain. He arrived in the Cariboo in the 1860s and set up business as a packer, quickly winning such a reputation for honesty and reliability that he continued to ply his trade until 1913.

Beaver Pass. He was after what locals called a "fool hen," what we would call a grouse. Guichon was en route from Williams Creek to Quesnellemouth when, about two miles beyond the Bloody Edwards' Ranch near Beaver Pass, he spotted the grouse at trailside (Edwards was an Englishman who earned his nickname by the frequent use of the adjective "bloody.")

Probably thinking that grouse would taste a whole lot better than the Barkerville staple of bacon and beans, Guichon sent a rock thumping into the breast of the bird, which toppled back, out of sight. So far, so good.

Head filled with thoughts of supper, he loped over to the scrub expecting to find the bird lying just beyond the branch. Nothing. As he groped about in the foliage for the small feathery body, his hand closed instead on an entirely different shape. He drew aside a screen of leaves. There lay the skeleton and a few fleshy remains of what had once been a human being.

Soon after the news of the body reached the Creek, Magistrate William Cox and Chief Constable William H. Fitzgerald left for the crime scene to hold an inquest on the remains. With them went a sufficient number of people to form a coroner's jury.

Establishing the cause of death was easy — there was a bullet hole in the back of the skull. They noted that the teeth were perfect in both jaws, although the lower and upper back molars were filled with gold. The clothing appeared undisturbed except that one of the pockets of the trousers had been turned inside out.

In other pockets were found a silver hunting case watch stamped with the maker's name, Joseph Tobias of Liverpool; a silver pencil case inscribed with the initials C.M.B; and a small clasp purse containing a few grains of fine gold wrapped in a piece of tea paper.

A sheath knife found near the feet of the remains had the initials C.M.B. carved into its handle, and there was also a new tin cup with the name C.M. Blessing scratched on the bottom.

The coroner's jury returned a verdict of willful murder against some person or persons unknown.

The news must have hit Moses like the blast from a stick of dynamite because he sped to the authorities with what he knew.

No this is not a spic and span cottage belonging to a miner, but a residence for the unruly - the Soda Creek Jail.

But Barry was even quicker. Police learned later that he had fled the Creek the day after Guichon's find was announced, taking an old fur trappers' trail that intercepted the Cariboo Wagon Road near Soda Creek on the Fraser River.

A warrant for Barry's arrest was sworn out, and on October 2 Special Constable John Howe Sullivan set out on horseback in pursuit. He arrived at Soda Creek the next day only to learn that, just a few hours before, Barry had left on the stagecoach south, booking himself through to Lytton, just north of Yale in the Fraser Canyon.

A few months earlier Barry would have been home free, but a telegraph line had just been installed and was being tested. Constable Sullivan had the presence of mind to ask the company to send an urgent message to police at Yale and Lytton, before continuing his chase.

Just twelve hours after the message was sent, the stage was

This undated view of Richfield shows something of the general chaos that prevailed, but there was a time when there would have been more tents than cabins in view.

intercepted at Yale (some reports say at Alexandra Bridge). Barry gave his name as James Corbett, but police arrested him anyway. He later said he had given a false name "for a lark" because he thought the officer was a newspaper reporter.

Constable Sullivan arrived on October 8 and took Barry into custody. The pair traveled back to Williams Creek on the stage, arriving on October 14. Sullivan said that throughout the journey Barry conducted himself well and didn't try to escape. However, in conversation with Sullivan, after being cautioned he had made several contradictory statements, one of the most significant being, first a claim, and then a denial, that he had money when he arrived at the Creek.

Barry also admitted having a pistol at Quesnellemouth, but said he sold it to Dutch Bill, the packer, to cover a gambling debt. They had been tossing for drinks at the 13 Mile Roadhouse en route to Williams Creek.

On October 16, a preliminary enquiry into the charge of murder was held before Mr. Cox in the log courthouse at Richfield, one mile upstream from Barkerville.

The Barkerville newspaper, *The Cariboo Sentinel,* told its readers that the prisoner stoutly maintained his innocence. But this wasn't enough. The weight of evidence from Moses and others who had seen Barry on the road to Williams Creek was sufficient for him to be held in custody for trial.

Police were now faced with the unenviable task of tracing other witnesses crucial to the prosecution case, and convincing them to stick around. Barry would take ten months to be brought to trial, but only two days to be condemned to death.

• • •

1. The *Enterprise* was packed north of Hells Gate in sections and reassembled to ply the upper Fraser River.
2. Some twentieth century newspaper accounts call him "Jack" or "John" Barry. These are incorrect. One newspaper account renders "Barry" as "Berry," a mistake copied from page six of the Barkerville County Court Record Book (which also doubled as the a police charge book) of October 14, 1866.

Chapter Two

Castles in the Air

The Cariboo was a magnet to men like Charlie Blessing and Del Moses. The two friends came from quite different backgrounds and yet their dreams and aspirations had them walking the same paths. One was a prospector and the other a barber, but the lure of gold enthralled them both. The veteran prospectors had a name for the process that lured the majority of men north. They called it "building castles in the air."

Imagine the daydreamers plodding north in the thousands, each one energized by dreams of the way gold would change their lives. Always in front of them, as though floating in the air, was the vision of bonanza — the "Big One" — the strike that would change things forever.

The gold seekers stepped on the Cariboo Wagon Road at Yale and plodded for 385 miles until they reached its end. Some were not physically capable of completing the journey; others, like Charlie, were taken by dangers along the way. Most were laden down by heavy packs. Some even pushed handcarts. Often their boots and the backs of their jackets were caked by pounds of sticky mud, the extra burden of which hastened their weariness — weariness, utter weariness — so great that for some, the time came when they fell and were too tired to get up again.

What did the trekkers find at the end of their journey? Most found a hard life with good, if unspectacular, rewards. Others found great riches. Some of the latter lost their riches almost as fast as they found them, and then flirted with Lady Luck in the belief that what they had done once, they could do again. Few succeeded the second time around. Thousands moved on to the next big strike, always one step behind the trailblazers and never quite able to be in the right place at the right time.

At the end of the Cariboo Wagon Road was Barkerville, a wild and woolly frontier town with its share of saloons, no-goods, dance hall gals and ladies of easy virtue. Just another mining town? Not really. Barkerville and the Cariboo were far more law abiding than comparable "rush" areas in the United States. Much of the credit for this has been given to the stern and uncompromising hand of Judge Matthew Baillie Begbie, who was to try James Barry and condemn him to death. But not everyone agreed with his rough and ready style of justice.

Probably the first tourists in the Cariboo were Viscount Milton and Dr. W.B. Cheadle, two Englishmen who would later write a best seller about their experiences.

Dr. Cheadle was told by one miner, "Well doctor, I've the greatest respect for both the professions of law and medicine; but it's a curious fact that in this creek last year we had neither lawyers nor doctors, and we lived without litigation and free from illness.

Lawyer Joseph Parks

One Joseph Parks, described as "an exceedingly clever lawyer," came to a soggy end when he tried to find a quick way home to Barkerville from a party in Richfield. Considering himself too drunk to travel, he either fell or climbed into a flume (water chute) and was swept away in a fast, furious, and ultimately final, flurry of spray. He was fished out of the pool at the bottom of the flume and taken to hospital where he died the next morning.

Judge Matthew Baillie Begbie seen resting outside his cabin in Richfield. He lived in New Westminster but as a circuit judge travelled throughout the region dispensing his brand of tough justice, sometimes from horseback.

This year there has been a large influx of both lawyers and doctors, and there has been nothing but lawsuits and death in this place!"

Business was so brisk that some of the more active lawyers were making $500 a day sorting out land titles and allegations of claim jumping, and collecting $25 for a single bill of sale on half a sheet of paper.

However, Barkerville's citizens came from all walks of life; and, while saloons abounded, there was also a theatre, a library, churches, sports clubs, musical groups, and a variety of other organizations that round out a community. Some men even brought their families with them.

How did this community, which was, by the standards of the day, law-abiding, react to the news of Charlie's murder? Quite simply, the discovery of his body created a sensation and provoked *The Sentinel* into producing some outraged editorials.

For example, consider what *The Sentinel* said on July 4, 1867, about the sentencing of Barry and Nikel Palsk, a native Indian who had also been found guilty of murder and was destined to hang on the same day as Barry.

Judge Begbie in a more formal setting in later years.

> We have never lived in any community where the extreme
> penalty of the law was inflicted, in which opinion ruled so
> completely against the prisoners, or where the punishment
> was more justly meted out as an expiation for the measure of
> their crimes.

Barry was said to have "evinced an amount of human depravity and
hardened villainy that makes one shudder to think that human beings,
with at least average intelligence like him, are to be found at large in
our midst. It is at least reassuring to think that in a British Colony, and
even in such an isolated portion of it as this, such wretches will not
be permitted the exercise of such horrible instincts with impunity."

Palsk's crime, though considered equally horrible, was "less
revolting to humanity inasmuch as the perpetrator was an unenlightened savage." The whole character of the deed, the writer said,
showed "the ignorant bloodthirsty savage throughout and remains
quite another phase from the black-hearted crimes of Barry."

In other words, the savage could be partly excused because he
knew no better, whereas Barry did. Indeed, the writer expressed agree-
ment with remarks by the judge and prosecutor that Barry was a prac-
ticed hand, familiar with crimes of the worst character. He elaborated:

> In Europe where such beings as Barry are unknown, or at least
> extremely rare, a great cry has been raised against the infliction of
> capital punishment. It is true that the punishment of death is a ter-
> rible alternative and should only be resorted to in cases like those
> under consideration. But we are firmly convinced that an all-wise
> Creator in the wonderful aid he renders to the arm of human jus-
> tice, signifies his wish that human retribution should be meted out
> to the criminal who embrues his hands in the blood of his fellow
> mortal, and we trust that no over-refined sentimentality will be
> allowed to Interfere with what appears to us to be the Divine Will.

If *The Sentinel* mirrored the thoughts of the community, Barkerville
wanted to see Barry hang. However, we should be careful how
much we read into the moral outrage of a single journalist. It is clear
though, from other things I have read, that Barkerville was bursting

with the same mix of hope and optimism that fired most pioneer towns. What is more, Barkerville considered itself to have something that many of the others lacked — the ability to survive beyond the gold. It did not want murderers as part of the dream.

Barkerville is still here and gold is still being produced in the region, but I wonder what those optimistic early writers would make of the fact that their town did go into decline and has survived only be becoming a provincial historical site.

Barkerville in Charlie's day had passed the first flush of gold fever and was settling down to secure its future. Most of the easy gold near the surface had gone and big mining companies were preparing to pursue the deeper deposits that were harder to win. Just as had happened with the Fraser Canyon strikes, some of the first wave of prospectors was moving further north to where discoveries in Alaska and the Yukon beckoned.

In 1866, the residents of Barkerville felt that they were not always being treated fairly by the colonial government. *The Sentinel's* editorial writer captured these sentiments when he said, "Our population, composed as it is of men from all over the globe, has exhibited an amount of endurance and patient suffering almost without parallel. We are taxed to an unbearable extent, over-ridden by the administrators of the law and treated with contempt when we have attempted to seek redress at the seat of government."

He asked, "Where else would you find another community prepared to go through what we have endured and still show obedience to the laws and respect to the government?"

At this time, the community had just sent two men south to New Westminster to plead for more "help and facilities" (Messrs. F. Laumeister and J. McLaren, according to *The Sentinel* of June 28, 1866). The people of Barkerville were confident that they could not be ignored forever because for a long time to come no other community would be able to contribute as much to the colony's collective wellbeing as they did with their gold. At the same time it was galling to see New Westminster booming from Cariboo gold whilst Barkerville languished.

The miner, until he has arrived at a section of country where he is likely to remain for some time, is the most careless fellow in the world with regard to Government and Law; he adapts himself with great facility however to the habits and customs of the people he dwells with, and hence legislators are apt to be misled, and believe him ready to bear any imposition and affliction, with the most imperturbable apathy. This is an error against which we would most seriously recommend everyone in authority to be on their guard; and we feel convinced that it will be so palpably apparent to our Government at New Westminster when the two gentlemen delegated by our citizens have made their representations, that immediate remedies will be applied to the evils, brought about by the proneness of the Government to fallacies now so completely exploded.

Earlier in the same editorial, *The Sentinel* said, "The Cariboo at this moment is the only place in the colony and elsewhere for that matter where a miner can earn his seven or eight dollars a day." They were not just talking about the summers, which could be rather short, but the entire year.

"The steady way our mineral wealth is being developed — particularly in contrast with the poor showings of the other mines which were supposed to throw us extremely in the shade — this had led many of our miners to look on the Cariboo as a home for years, if not permanently." The writer added that the legislators "shouldn't make the mistake of thinking they can get away with ignoring us because we are just another mining town that won't be around for long. Barkerville is here to stay."

Technically, he was right. Although often billed as a Western ghost town, Barkerville has always been home to someone. True, its heyday was over long before the end of the nineteenth century, and its viability received another jolt when attention switched to the lode gold strike in nearby Wells in the 1930s. True, that by the 1950s there were only a few holdouts left; but they saw the town through to 1958 when the preservation work began. Because of them, Barkerville's supporters can say truthfully that it never was a ghost town — even though ghosts have been sighted in some of its old buildings![1]

In the early years, travelers approached Barkerville not from the north as they do today, but from the south. This brought them through Richfield where the gold was first discovered in quantity (about $1,000 to the foot). Early photographs show 1860s Richfield as a sea of mud, gravel, tents and shanties. The hillsides appear as though stripped clear of trees by a bomb blast. Today, the land has long since healed itself and the only sign of Richfield's inhabitation is the white weatherboard courthouse that replaced the original log building.

When Barkerville sprang into being around Billy Barker's claim some two kilometers away in the lower canyon, it looked much the same as early Richfield. However, this was where the serious gold was. By Charlie's day, many of the tents had given way to rough, mud-chinked log cabins and there was not only a bustling main street of "permanent" frame buildings, but a lane, or back street as well.

Clamor and confusion reigned everywhere, not just in the town itself, but also along the tangle of creeks in the region where men toiled. Shafts, sluices, water wheels and mine workings of various kinds surrounded the buildings in the town. Much of the water would have been used to power pumps and other mine "engines."

Williams Creek was harried from one side of the valley to the other, not only in its present course, but also along other channels it had worn in the geological past. Some of the shafts went down by as much as sixty feet in pursuit of these old channels, and men worked by candlelight in chilly, waist-deep water, praying that the pumps would hold. Little wonder that the average age of those interred in the cemetery on the hill was a mere thirty-one years. Poor Charlie was right on the number.

Barkerville was noisy. The clang of metal on metal would have testified to men busily engaged in their various pursuits. Axe blows, the thump of picks, the sharper crack of hammers and the rasp of saws echoed down from the hills on either side of the settlement. No bomb blast here, just a steady stripping away of hillside trees to provide timber for buildings and posts to shore up mine shafts.

Barkerville was messy. The main street was crossed frequently by overhead water pipes, made of wood and wrapped at the joints. Nevertheless, plenty of water escaped to drip down on the heavily rutted roadway. Cattle were sometimes driven down the main street, and on more festive occasions horse races were held.

Boardwalks on either side of the street lifted pedestrians out of the mire, but moving about must still have been a contest with mud, snow, or dust, depending on the season. A complicating factor was that all of the buildings were on piles to escape the frequent flooding of the valley. Many of them settled into the soft ground, making passage along the boardwalks a hippetty-hop progression from one level to the other.

Most of the buildings were unpainted, their timbers bleached bare like old bones in the sun. A few essayed bold facades in optimistic statements about the future, but most were modest, simple structures designed to get a business under way as quickly as possible. In just such a building (the former Dixon store), Del Moses set up shop. He was able to look out his windows to watch the stage pull up across the street, or simply to observe the rest of his world as it passed by. Much of what he saw found its way into his journals, even mundane observations about the weather or the number and purposes of passengers on the stage.

Barkerville would have been an olfactory experience too in those days, with the heady mix of mud, animal droppings, sweat, and the more pleasant tang of fresh-sawn lumber. Rough it was, ready it may have been, but everywhere were signs of life.

Barkerville as "place" is only part of the picture though. The people who inhabit a town contribute just as much to its character, and Barkerville certainly had its share of eccentrics.

Today we are still mining from their experiences a legacy of laughter and admiration that teaches us much about the human spirit. Already, some of their stories have achieved the status of legend.

For example, nearly everyone familiar with the Cariboo has a story about Judge Begbie. One tells of how, while staying in a hotel at Clinton, he overheard a group of men threatening to shoot him for convicting one of their friends. Did the good judge, esteemed as a man of action, come out guns blazing? Nope. He emptied his chamber pot over their heads.

In another story, while on a visit to Barkerville, Begbie, who had an interest in natural history, picked some wild oats while out walking in a meadow and was examining them in an attempt to determine the fertility of the soil.

"Sowing or reaping Judge?" asked a local wag.

"Neither, my friend," Begbie replied. "The man who comes to this country to sow his wild oats will find so many difficulties besetting him that he will quickly abandon the project — you understand?"

That just about summed up the philosophy that would help him rise to become the first Chief Justice of British Columbia when it joined the Confederation of Canada as a province. However, in the twilight years of his career, his outspokenness did not sit well with "modern" lawyers further removed from pioneer time. For example, he once called a jury a pack of horse thieves and told another that he hoped the man they had just acquitted would make them his next victims.

Gold Is Where You Find It

Nearly every creek within a twenty-mile radius of Barkerville was said to be gold bearing, some more so than others.

The first strikes were made in Williams Creek at Richfield (named after "Dutch Bill" William Dietz), but most of this was surface gold that was played out by 1864. Emphasis then switched to Barkerville about a mile and a quarter (two kilometers) away in the "lower canyon." There, gold was found at three different levels:

- Some, as in Richfield, was found on the surface;
- A better yield was found lower down on a false bedrock of hard, blue clay;
- Those who dug deeper to the gravel of old creek beds on true bedrock were rewarded with the best yields of all.

Much of the richer strikes were at depths of between fifty and sixty feet. For the miners, this meant working in unpleasant and sometimes deadly conditions. Bone-chilling cold, water up to waist deep, and the dreaded Cariboo slum — oozing, semi-liquid clay sludge — all took a grim toll. The average age of those buried in the Barkerville Cemetery during the rush years was a mere thirty-one.

Perhaps no one will ever know how much gold was taken out of the Cariboo. Sometimes figures of $40-50 million worth (in nineteenth century values when gold was $15–16 an ounce) are suggested, but other sources claim that as yields were often "fudged" to avoid paying taxes; the true figure was much higher.

Barkerville's Masonic Hall (right) was a bold presence in the string of buildings along the town's main street. The Lodge had a strong membership judging by the photograph below.

The Barkerville Dramatic Society, seen here outside the Theatre Royal, provided a welcome diversion from the drudgery of the miners' work.

Some of the famous Barkerville mud is evident in this view of the main street showing at extreme right what appears to be the Express (stage coach) office operated by Francis Jones Barnard. Moses the barber was once said to have his saloon opposite the Express office, enabling him to record the comings and goings in his daily journal.

Another character was the burly American miner, Bill Diller, who boasted: "I'm not going home 'til I've found my weight in gold." Diller, who weighed 240 pounds, made good on his boast and also got enough gold for his 120-pound dog and quite a bit more besides. On one incredible day he brought out 102 pounds of gold from his 100-foot claim a few yards from the main street of Barkerville. For weeks his mine declared a dividend every Sunday of $10,000 a share.

A young man from Vermont named Henry Fuller Davis arrived in Barkerville too late to stake a claim on prime ground, but was not deterred. Although illiterate, he knew his figuring. After careful pacing he estimated that the Steele claim and the neighboring Abbott and Jourdan claim were improperly staked. The authorities agreed and allowed Davis to work a twelve-foot strip of land between the two properties.

Twelve-Foot Davis, as he was soon known, won $12,000 from his mini-claim before selling out to a man who in turn also made $12,000. The property was again sold, to an industrious group of Chinese miners who earned another $25,000.

J.B. Malamon, a violinist who had played with the Paris Opera, made his living in Barkerville not as a miner, but as a carpenter. In 1879 when he and O.G. Travailot lay dying in the Cariboo Hospital, he wagered fifty cents as to who would go first.

Near dawn, Malamon said in a clear voice, "Captain Travailot, you win, I lose. I die now." With these words still ringing in the air, his head fell forward.

The merest whisper of a gold strike could set off a mini-stampede. This was the case when a group of prospectors came into the rush town of Antler, trying desperately to appear casual. Not a word was said about the strike they had just made, and after buying supplies they took a circuitous route back just in case they were followed. When they reached their claim they pitched tents, ate an evening meal and prepared to retire for the night. One of the men, wise in the ways of this part of the world, stepped out of his tent and shouted, "Is everyone here yet?"

"Not quite," came an answering cry from the darkness. "There are still a few spread out along the trail." Sure enough, by next morning there were tents all around them.

Numerous stories are told of the antics and excesses of successful miners. One fellow, determined to share his good fortune, announced that he would stand everyone a glass of champagne. Annoyed when he ran out of drinkers, he had the saloonkeeper line the bar with glasses of the bubbly beverage and smashed the lot. Another miner called for a barrel of champagne, cracked open the top and washed his feet in it.

Another story tells of two miners, Pat Murray and Black Martin, who were gambling in Scotch Jeannie's saloon one Christmas. "Well," said Murray, "I'll shake you the dice for all the wine that Jeannie has." Martin lost. Jeannie's stock was sixty-four bottles, which, at the going rate of an ounce of gold per bottle, was worth more than $1,300. What the heck, it was only money!

The Cariboo gold seekers entered a world of back-breaking, joint-popping labor often carried out deep underground in water or the dreaded Cariboo "slum" — a waxy, almost liquid mud whose chill could leech your life away. In some instances the miners could be as much as fifty or sixty feet down, following buried stream beds, hoping to strike gold in the sand, silt, and fine gravel. However, if there was still enough water present to saturate these materials, they could become "slum," which flowed like a heavy pudding batter into the spaces where the miners toiled.

Work, work, work, day after day on a diet of Cariboo turkey and Cariboo strawberries — bacon and beans — unless you lived in a boarding house. Then it was the turn of the lady of the house to toil, serving up as many as five types of meat at breakfast to give the men a good start for what lay ahead.

In 1863 a journalist describing the clutter of hastily erected buildings that made up the more substantial part of Richfield, penned an almost poetic impression of the hard slog.

> In and out of this nest the human ants poured all day and night, for in wet-sinking the labour must be kept up without ceasing all through the 24 hours, Sunday included. It was a curious sight to look down the creek at night and see each shaft with its little fire and its lanterns, and the dim ghostly figures gliding about from darkness to light, while an occasional hut was illuminated by some weary labourer returning from his nightly toil.

Four out of five of the miners were Americans, many from California, and among them were the veterans chuckling at tales of greenhorns "building castles in the air."

But in the Cariboo, as elsewhere, storekeepers, packers, lawyers and saloonkeepers who brought the trappings of civilization to the wilderness made some of the fortunes. Even Del Moses contributed far more than haircuts and shaves.

In those times, a company miner worked for wages of $7–10 a day. An average meal at a restaurant or roadhouse was likely to cost $2.50. A bottle of wine cost an ounce of gold (then worth about $16). A drink and a dance with a girl in one of the saloons cost $1. Tobacco cost about $5 per pound. The going rate for staples in 1862 was:

> flour $1.00–1.25 a pound;
> salt $1.20 for five pounds;
> bacon $1.50–1.75 a pound;
> sugar $1.50 a pound;
> coffee and tea $2.50 and $3.00 per tin, respectively;
> candles $3.00 a dozen;
> matches $5.00 for a dozen boxes;
> potatoes $90 for 100 pounds;
> eggs cost up to $8.00 a dozen.

A good pair of India rubber boots was likely to set a miner back $50; and really up-market goods such as stoves and big mirrors were $500–700. Glass was pricey too. The 8x10-inch panes in the windows of the old Richfield Courthouse cost $3 each. (Incidentally, Barry was suspected of stealing a pair of gumboots, but the charge was dropped for want of evidence.)

Some of the prices fell when the 385-mile Cariboo Wagon Road was opened in 1865 and freighting became big business. It is believed that the heaviest single item brought north was a 40,000-pound boiler hauled by a sixteen-horse outfit. However, pianos and billiard tables were also packed in to goldfield saloons.

The men who drove the teams took great pride in their expertise, which could be measured by the height of their trouser bottoms. A man in charge of a two-horse team would turn his pant legs up one roll. Four horses entitled him to two rolls, and so on. As some of the three-wagon outfits were drawn by sixteen horses, their drivers might as well have been wearing shorts!

The real elite were the stagecoach drivers who assumed the authority of ships' captains over their passengers, sitting at the head of the table at road houses and driving with great dash when there was an audience. At other times, the horses maintained a steady six miles per hour and were exchanged at way stations every eighteen miles.

However, most of the early travelers had no choice but to walk the Wagon Road. Many died before they reached the goldfields, and others endured almost unbelievable trials.

For example, consider the case of Edward (Ned) Stout who was in San Francisco when he heard word of a gold strike in the British Territory to the north. He and some friends hired a schooner to take them to Bellingham in what is now Washington State. There they built two flat-bottomed scows and, using oars and sails, made their way to the Fraser River in southwest British Columbia (then known as New Caledonia or simply British Territory). They traveled upstream as far as Fort Yale and the Fraser Canyon, arriving on May 20, 1858.

That summer Stout was one of a party of twenty-six men who fought a running battle with Indians who had been much provoked by American prospectors. By the time they were rescued, only four were still alive, one of them Ned, although with seven arrows in him he was more dead than alive. During the early stages of the battle, the Indians had been putting rattlesnake venom on their arrow tips, but by the time Stout was first wounded, they had run out of the poison.

The hardy prospector, who took pride in being teetotal, recovered in time to join the Cariboo Rush further north and participate in the discovery of the fabulous wealth of Williams Creek. There he made a major strike in what is now known as Stout's Gulch, near Barkerville. Later he settled in Yale until his death at the age of ninety-nine.

Prospectors and miners in Barkerville had a year-round battle against the forces of nature, but there were other natural forces active on the goldfields. One of the most formidable was Madame Fanny Bendixen who operated the Parlor Saloon, among others, and supervised the activities of the dancing girls known as "Hurdies." Charlie's killer, James Barry, was one of their regular customers.

A contemporary writer, much impressed with Madame Bendixen, as she liked to be known, described her as being "in great form, indeed enormous, vast, of undiscoverable girth, though she was always of goodly diameter."

When a miner danced with one of the Hurdies he had to buy a drink for himself and a fruit juice for the girl. She got fifty cents from the price of each drink the next morning when the bartender had totted up the tabs. If the miner misbehaved, he had the chilling prospect of a personal interview with the formidable Madame Bendixen.

Most of her girls were from good Dutch or German families and could best be described as poor, but honest. They too were seeking to find a place for themselves in a new world. Fanny decked them out in cotton print skirts with red waistbands and half-mourning headdresses resembling the topknots of tom turkeys.

The dresses had a bell shape, which encouraged the miners in a peculiar and highly energetic dance known as "ringing the bell." The girls were grasped around the waist and swung high off the ground so that their feet (the clappers of the bells) almost touched the ceiling. He who could swing his girl the highest was judged the winner of the contest.

Where did they get the name "Hurdy" or "Hurdy Gurdy"? Some say it was from the type of music played, and others point out that "hurdy" was a good Scottish term for hips and bottoms.

In any event, James Anderson, known as the Scottish bard of Barkerville, wrote and sang his opinion of the Hurdies. He described them as having tight dresses and hearts as hard as flint. The dollar was their only love, he said, and "They left the creek wi' lots of gold, danced frae our lads sae clever, O." The chorus was:

> "Bonny are the Hurdies, O!
> The German Hurdy-Gurdies, O!
> The daftest hour that e'er I spent
> Was dancin' wi' the Hurdies, O!"

Dancing was a big-time entertainment in the Cariboo. To be sure, there was horse racing, prize fighting, gambling, boozing, a library, and a host of theatrical offerings, but dancing was something else.

Take for example, the town of Clinton, the gateway to the Cariboo. In 1868 when it had only a handful of occupants, hotel proprietors Joe and Mary Smith decided to hold a ball. That's right, a ball! And a grand one it was, too. There was actually a whole week of celebrations.

Camels North!

Just about the last thing a prospector would expect to encounter on the trail north was a caravan of camels — and that was one of the main reasons for the failure of what became known as "The Dromedary Express."

In 1862 a syndicate (Frank Laumeister, Adam Heffley, and Henry Ingram) bought twenty-three Bactrian (two-humped) camels from the American Camel Company in Nevada. The plan was to use them to freight goods to and from the Cariboo goldfields.

On paper, the idea made sense. Camels could carry about 800 pounds compared to a mule's 300 pounds, and were expected to double or even triple the mule's limit of about fifteen miles a day. As a bonus, they could do this while going without food and water for long periods. What is more, they were expected to thrive in the hot, dry Cariboo summers.

So where did it all go wrong? There were three main reasons. The camels were bossy, they stank, and their feet were better suited to sand than the rock and hardpan of the Cariboo trails (to say nothing of mud and snow).

The smell of the camels was so rank and strange that it spooked other animals and rival pack trains. The dislike was mutual because the camels bit and kicked anything that crossed their paths, even oxen. Attempts were made to overcome this antipathy by bathing the camels in perfumed water, but a whiff of camel was still olfactory dynamite. Soon, the other packers had started a petition asking for camels to be banned.

In the end it was the footing that put paid to The Dromedary Express, even though attempts were made to fit the camels with boots made of canvas and rawhide. The camel brigade was disbanded in 1864 and the last of the camels was said to have died near Grande Prairie in the northern Okanagan in 1905.

They were capable of spooking man and beast until the last though. One prospector earned himself the nickname "Grizzly Morris" when he shot and killed what he thought was a bear in the bush only to discover that he had bagged a camel.

People came from hundreds of miles away and the Smiths judged it such a success that it became an annual affair. Each year guests would arrive from as far away as San Francisco and Chicago. At the time of writing the ball was still going strong and had become a major tourist attraction.

On September 16, 1868, some fancy footwork was essayed by a miner at Barkerville whilst trying to steal a kiss from a girl in Barry and Adler's Gazelle Saloon. As she attempted to evade him, the girl bumped into a stovepipe and sent a shower of sparks flying into the tinder-dry roof. That moment of hot passion burned the saloon — and Barkerville — to the ground. Friends of the would-be kisser concealed his identity, as they feared he would be lynched if he were found out.

In all, 116 buildings worth $700,000 were destroyed, among them Del Moses' barbershop. He was back in business quickly though. Indeed, *The Sentinel* reported that within a week of the fire, thirty new buildings had been erected. The rebuilding of Barkerville began while its ashes were still warm and today it stands as a provincial historic site peopled by actors, entertainers and more than 200,000 visitors a year. Once, thousands of people like Charlie and Del came from all over the world to take gold away from the Cariboo; now the tourists are bringing it back.

• • •

1. The restoration of Barkerville as a living museum, an historic town, seeks to recreate the environment of 1869–85. Street performers, who bring to life many of the events and personalities of the past, enhance this image. However, just as the streets are cleaner and the town more groomed, so too are the stories and images more polished. I greatly enjoy the experience they provide, but worry that something is being lost, that all the generalizing and sanitizing dilute the essence. Barkerville still has its "living history", but is in danger of becoming a theme park. The picture of Barkerville I carry within me is of a roaring town, a rowdy town — one where fortunes could be won or lost overnight — rough, rude, and ready, but essentially law-abiding.

Some sought their gold directly while others earned their "treasure" by serving the miners as in this Cariboo Road saloon.

Around 1866 Barkerville had at least 12 saloons - a testament to the miners' thirst! This is Bill Forrest's Saloon.

Yes, there was gold there and a lot of it, but usually it didn't come easily, be it for the lone man with a rocker (right) or a gang (below). These were hard times that demanded hard men - physically hard at least.

They worked at the edge of the wilderness and sometimes the wilderness came calling - as in the case of this moose calf.

The scourge of wooden buildings was fire. After its destruction in 1868, Barkerville was determined that it wouldn't happen again. This is the Williams Creek Fire Brigade in the 1890s.

Barkerville, September 17, 1868, the day after fire ripped through the town. Buildings worth about $700,000 were reduced to ash. The only house left standing was the one shown below.

As time went by, refinements eased the way north, such as this bridge over the Thompson River. The Thompson is the largest tributary of the Fraser River which it joins at Lytton.

This was typical of the cabins miners built to rest in from their labours. They were often damp, dark and smoky (See reference on page 56).

Sometimes the miners dossed down in crude bunkhouses not too different from the long houses of their ancestors in medieval times.

For some miners, tents were their home away from home. Many went south to winter over in the gentler climes of New Westminster or Victoria and returned to their diggings in spring.

Chapter Three

Charlie's Last Day

We will probably never know why Charlie Blessing allowed himself to be talked into accompanying Barry on the last leg of his journey to the goldfields. In spite of his protestations about not wanting to go broke on the trail, he'd rashly shown everyone in the bar of the Occidental that he still had plenty of money. He and Del Moses had shared their misgivings about traveling with Barry. Their gut instincts said, "Don't do it." What is more, Charlie had initially decided to heed these inner promptings.

All Charlie had to do was hold off for another day or so until Del had recovered the $10 he'd lent out the season before. Then he'd have had a pleasant and proven traveling companion every step of the way to Van Winkle. Charlie had thought so highly of Del's company that he'd overcome his impatience and waited for him just north of Yale. Why not again?

Surely Charlie's pals at Van Winkle would have waited another forty-eight hours for him? If he really was worried that they might think he was not coming and give his place to someone else, there were several points en route from Yale where he could have sent a letter ahead to say that he was almost there.

The most likely reason for his change of mind was that Barry sweet-talked him. Del described Charlie as a shy man, almost timid, while Barry, who, by his own admission, associated with men in the penitentiary at New Westminster, was anything but. One can see him overwhelming Charlie with sheer force of personality, coupled with a glibness of tongue. Like most con men he could be charming when necessary, and he was quite capable of baiting his trap with an approach like this.

"Well now, Mr. Blessing, you say you don't want to go broke. Then why pay for another night in the hotel when you don't have to? I know a place where I'll be staying free tonight. Why don't you bunk down with me? We can make an early start in the morning and you'll be with your mates in Van Winkle that much quicker."

It is possible that Barry had not decided to kill Charlie at this stage. No evidence was produced to show that anyone else stayed with them, so we can assume that Barry was alone with Charlie, allowing Barry to "work" on Charlie psychologically. It's likely that, initially, Barry simply planned to con Charlie out of his money.

Witnesses said later that Barry had been trying to borrow money from others in the bar and on the trail. To a con man on the make, Charlie would have seemed a perfect target. The only problem was his more trail-wise friend. Barry's first task, therefore, was to separate Charlie and Del. This was most likely accomplished the next day when Barry and Charlie were seen deep in conversation on the bench outside the hotel.

Once they were alone in the house, Barry probably would have been too cunning to make a simple demand for money. He might have first dropped a few sly hints about being broke and then followed up with a seemingly casual request. Almost certainly, Charlie would have refused — after all if he had dossed down in the abandoned house to save money, why would he give some away to such a dubious character?

Barry would have hidden his annoyance; if Charlie walked out on him at this point he'd get nothing. Sometimes when you have a fish on the hook you have to play it for a while. Barry would be with Charlie for about forty miles to Van Winkle, so he knew there would be other opportunities to steal from him, or do him harm. Very few people testified later to having seen them on the trail, so they must have been alone together for miles at a time.

How long would Barry's patience have lasted? Probably not long. Once they were alone on the open road, if Charlie kept saying "no," Barry's reserve would have soon given way to anger.

About twenty-six miles from Quesnellemouth, the decision point was reached. Barry lured Charlie off the trail on some pretext and shot him in the back of the head. He then took what he wanted, leaving behind everything marked with Charlie's name. There was only one identifiable thing he is believed to have taken — an odd-shaped Californian gold nugget that Charlie had fixed to a pin and referred to as his lucky piece.

Popular stories have Charlie displaying the pin at the Occidental and even suggest that Moses might have stolen it there, but no evidence was given to this effect, and the diligent *Sentinel* reporter made no mention of it either. Even more stories have circulated in the years since about how the pin surfaced in Barkerville, so the account that follows repeats what can be proven. Interestingly, Charlie had some less conspicuous gold with him — the twist of flakes in tea paper — but this was left for the coroner to find. Perhaps Barry overlooked it, or maybe he decided it wasn't worth bothering with.

Barry may have hoodwinked Charlie, but he had fallen far short of convincing Del to trust him. Not only did Del try to talk his friend out of going with Barry, he worried about him so much that he went to the house early the next morning for another try. He was too late.

There is a saying that hindsight is the only perfect vision, but it can be cruel too. In a case such as this, the personal recriminations must have come to Del, unbidden: "Perhaps if I'd tried a bit harder to convince Charlie…Maybe I shouldn't have worried about collecting on the loan…Perhaps if I'd gone to the house earlier, and maybe even stayed there with them, this terrible thing would never have happened."

The steps for Del were, first, his initial misgivings about Barry; second, his relief that Charlie had decided to wait for him; and third, the return of his misgivings when Charlie said he had changed his mind and would go on ahead with Barry. Del's apprehension was still there when he called at the empty house the next morning, and stayed with him all the way to Van Winkle. When enquiries there produced no sign of Charlie, his anxiety gave way to alarm.

There was no doubt in Del Moses' mind that something had happened to his Chummy, as he called Blessing. He was fairly certain that Barry was responsible for his friend's disappearance, but there was nothing he could prove. All he knew was that Barry and Charlie had left Quesnellemouth together, and now, here was a better-dressed Barry in Barkerville denying any knowledge of Charlie's whereabouts.

In the meantime, Del had a business to set up and run. First, he found a temporary place to stay (Dixon's shop) and he liked it so much that he secured the lease. In an odd comment on how certain things were hard to come by in the pioneer town, he wound strips of red flannel around what would become his barber's pole instead of using red paint. Then, on June 11, 1866, *The Sentinel* made the formal announcement that W.D. Moses had just leased "the premises lately occupied by D.J. Dixon in Barkerville where he intends carrying on his old business of barber and hairdresser. His arrangements are not yet completed for supplying his hair Invigorator. He invites a call from his old friends and patrons."

No doubt shaggy-headed clients from the previous season soon sought him out, and before long it was business as usual. Another advertisement, in *The Sentinel* of June 25, advised that the Invigorator was now available.

PREVENTION IS BETTER THAN CURE
Moses' Hair Invigorator

TO PREVENT BALDNESS, restore hair that has fallen off or become thin, and to cure effectually Scurf or Dandruff. It will also relieve the Headache, and give the hair a darker and glossy color, and the free use of it will keep both the hair and the skin in a healthy state. Ladies will find the Invigorator a great addition to toilet, both in consideration of the delicate and agreeable perfume, and the great facility it affords in dressing the hair, which when moist with it, can be dressed in any required form, so as to preserve its place, whether plait or in curls. When used on children's heads, it lays the foundation for a good head of hair. Prepared only by W.D. Moses, Barkerville, Williams Creek.

In a marketing ploy that would not be out of place today, Del added several signed testimonials from satisfied users. The Invigorator advertisement might be a mere curiosity today but for the mention of women and children. Clearly, there were sufficient of both in Barkerville for Del to identify them as potential customers. This reinforces Barkerville's claim to being a true town and not just another mining camp.

An informal survey conducted in April the following year listed the various businesses in town. There were twelve saloons, ten stores, three shoemakers, three restaurants, three lodging houses, two bank agencies, two drug stores, two watchmakers, two brewers, two carpenter's shops, a printing office, a paint shop, a butcher's stall, the Express Office (stagecoach), a public library, a clothing store, and a public stable. I've also read of a blacksmith operating in the town, but am not sure whether the smithy would be included in the "ten stores" or whether it was part of the stables. The blacksmith was said to have had a small black dog called Boss that was always getting into fights. Sadly, Boss died in the fire of 1868.

The year before the survey, the library was situated in nearby

John Angus Cameron

Cameronton was named after John Angus Cameron who was fated to discover the Cariboo's second richest claim, but lose his daughter and wife in the process. His young daughter sickened and died soon after arriving in the harsh Cariboo environment, and his wife, Sophia, succumbed to typhoid a few months later. Cameron eventually lost his great riches in Ontario and returned to Barkerville to try again, but died penniless in 1888.

Cameronton, but it was moved into Barkerville proper in 1867. Williams Creek was then actually a grouping of three towns: Richfield, sometimes known as Upper Town, Barkerville or Mid-Town, and Cameron's Town, the Lower Town, which became Camerontown and then Cameronton. Eventually Richfield faded away, and Barkerville swallowed up Cameronton.

The cost of renting a portion of a house in Barkerville in 1869 was $100 a month. Building your own house was likely to set you back $3,500. In the declining Richfield, houses cost only $1,500, or could be rented for around $20–30 a month.

Home for many people though was a log cabin chinked with mud and moss and roofed with wooden shingles. Most likely it was only ten or twelve square feet. The interior would be dark and smoky, and in damp weather frequently uncomfortable. Heavy snowfalls often knocked over the tin chimneys, which added to the discomfort.

Although Barkerville might have been relatively law abiding, men were jealous and protective of their gold. Often they would bury their gold in tins beneath the floors of their cabins, or even tote it around with them until they had enough to redeem. And the lust for gold brought about other unpleasantness in town. Just as in most areas today, there were minority groups fighting for recognition, in particular, black people and Chinese. Remember, too, *The Sentinel's* description of the native Indian Nikel Palsk as an "unenlightened savage." It was clear that many white men considered they had more right to the gold claims than those in ethnic minorities.

Del Moses appears to have been well regarded in the Cariboo and fit into the community well in spite of his color, but he was working in what was perhaps seen as a necessary service occupation. Had he gone out after gold, things might have been different.

On the same page as Del's June 25 advertisement is a letter to the editor by "Colored Miner" who asked three questions:

- FIRST — Have we as colored men the right to pre-empt ground for mining purposes?
- SECOND — Have we any rights in common with white men?

- THIRD — Why were our interests taken from us and given to white men?

"Colored Miner" explained that he had bought an interest in the Davis company claim and expended $2,900 before receiving one cent back. The dividends he had received since had gone to paying his debts in the colony. Now, just at the time he was about to be rewarded, he had been deprived of that portion of the Davis claim that would pay.

> I have taken some pains to spread abroad the equality, we as colored men had, in the laws in an English colony," he said, "and am proud to say I have found no difference until now. Poor Marshall lost his life coming to Cariboo to look after his small interest in the Davis co'y, the only pittance he had left after 6 years hard work in this colony, and the only means of support for his family. His wife and four children are more in need of the money than those to whom it was given. There are about fifty colored men in and about Cariboo, the greater proportion of whom are miners, and the quicker we know our position in this colony the better for us.

The editor added a note to the letter stating that it had been hoped that discussion on this topic would have ceased with the decision of

The Chinese Presence

There was a strong Chinese presence in Barkerville from the beginning, and several members of this community came to be numbered among the pioneer town's most prominent and respected citizens. But, in a new world, links with the old were often hard to sever.

The Chinese community had its own cemetery on the hillside above the canyon through which Williams Creek ran. Every seven years, the bodies were disinterred so that old men could clean the bones. These were then shipped back to China for reburial in the homeland where it was hoped the spirits of the deceased would find greater peace.

Typical Chinese quarters.

Chinese prospectors were highly industrious, often winning good returns from claims abandoned by others.

the Marshall case and the matter be let drop. However, "we consider a great injury has been done to men whose rights have been outraged, by the one-sided decision given by a Supreme Court Judge in a British colony."

The writer considered it unnecessary to state in answer to "Colored Miner's" first two questions that the mining laws of the colony made no distinction as to the color of a man's skin, adding, "it is only with the administration of them that we take exception..."

"The laws may say one thing, but the Chief Justice says another, and we must grin and bear his 'ipse dixit' having no other recourse left. The Judge has given as his reasons for depriving "Colored Miner" of his claim, that it was an act of wisdom and expediency, justified by the circumstances of his, 'Colored Miner's,' knowledge of the jump; which singular to say, although it was not established to the satisfaction of the jury, was quite clear to the learned Judge."

Did this mean that Judge Begbie considered the colored miners to be unenlightened savages also?

On June 28, a similar case was reported, this one involving Chinese miners. Three days earlier, the Gold Commissioner's Court had convened before Mr W.G. Cox and heard a number of cases, one of which was that of Ah Wa and Co. vs John Williams, R. Booth and Jas. Wooten. According to *The Sentinel:*

> This suit was brought requiring defendants to show cause why they should not be ejected from plaintiffs' claim and plaintiffs put in possession. The defendants jumped the Chinamen's ground in the belief that they had no License and had not recorded; the Chinamen however proved their title. The Commissioner took occasion, while giving judgement for plaintiffs, to severely reprimand defendants, who had pulled out the Chinamen's stakes, against the repetition of such an offence, as it was deemed by the mining laws felony and would be punished accordingly.

Now here was a victory for the minority and a triumph for justice in early Barkerville. Who can say now why the men jumped the Chinese claim that had been staked and filed legally. The nasty implication is that they thought they could get away with it because their opponents were "only Chinamen."

"Wild and woolly" the Cariboo frontier might have been, but there are several accounts of men used to lawless behavior elsewhere being brought up short by their fellow citizens' attempts to make Barkerville a "real town."

But, walking about the streets of this real town was now one James Barry, gambler, dancer with the Hurdies, and a constant reminder to Del Moses of his unresolved questions about the disappearance of Charles Morgan Blessing.

Chapter Four

The Body in the Bush

News of the discovery of Charlie's body was received in Barkerville on the evening of Tuesday, September 25, 1866, nearly four months after he went missing. *The Sentinel* reported the discovery under the headline "Probable Murder" in its Thursday edition, but long before then the town was in an uproar, and from this period comes one of the most telling indicators of Barry's guilt.

Consider the facts. How many people knew the identity of the dead man? There is no indication that the initial report on Tuesday night included the name scratched on the belongings found with the body. Members of the coroner's jury would have found out eventually, but they didn't see the body until Saturday morning of that week and couldn't have brought the news back to Barkerville much before Sunday. Joseph Guichon would have long since passed through Quesnellemouth with his pack train.

That leaves only two people who had first-hand knowledge of the dead man's likely identity: Del Moses and James Barry. Now consider their reaction times.

Barbershops are usually hotbeds of gossip, so if a likely name for the dead man was given in the first announcement, Del was almost certain to have heard. However, he did not react until he saw a second report *The Sentinel* published on October 1, four days later. Before then he almost certainly worried that the dead man might have been Charlie, but he had no proof.

James Barry, on the other hand, did not wait for confirmation. The day after the news about the body reached town, and the day before the first report in *The Sentinel,* he packed his bags and fled. At this point the coroner hadn't even left to inspect the body.

The Sentinel's first report, published the day after Barry hit the trail for Soda Creek, made no mention of a name. It said little more than could have been gleaned from Guichon's message:

> Information was received on Tuesday evening, by the magistrate here, that the body of a man has been found in the woods about a mile below Edwards' ranch, near Beaver Pass.
>
> It would appear from what we could learn that the discovery was quite accidental. A packer going along the road shot at and wounded a grouse[1] and, in his endeavor to find the bird, had to leave the road for a few yards, where he unexpectedly discovered the remains of a man in a very advanced state of decomposition, the body being almost devoid of flesh and unrecognizable. The head rested on a coat, and the flesh on the lower side of the face still remained; a hole was observed in the skull, which is supposed to have been the effect of a bullet, and from the position of the body it is evident that the man came to his death by foul means.
>
> From the decomposed state of the body the deed must have been committed over a month ago. The body has not yet been identified, but it is more than probable that the clothes which still remain on it may lead to its identity. On the return of Mr. Cox, who proceeds to the spot this morning, we will be enabled to gather further particulars of this mysterious affair.

The promised "further particulars" were published on October 1,

1866, in an article that said Mr. Cox had left Barkerville on Friday, September 28 and the next morning reached the murder site. The newspaper report of his findings was what caused Del Moses to go to the authorities with his information. Barry would not have seen it because he had left town already. This second report moves the murder scene closer to the Bloody Edwards' ranch, describing it as "being distant nearly half a mile" below the ranch at a point where the Wagon Road intersected the old trail.

Mr. Cox swore in his jury before beginning his examination of the remains, which, according to *The Sentinel,* "they found lying in a hole into which the body must have been thrown after the murder had been committed." This time *The Sentinel* reported no "fleshy remains" but said nothing remained of the body but a "mere skeleton." They noted that the entry hole for the bullet was on the back of the skull and interpreted the absence of an exit hole as conclusive proof that the shot must have come from behind.

No mention is made of the bullet being found inside the skull, but it is possible that the bullet exited through an eye socket, or rolled out of the skull which had been moved some three or four yards from the rest of the body. Later police methods, with ballistic sciences well advanced, would have required the area to be scoured in a grid search for the slug and other clues. In any event, the murder weapon was never found, and there is no evidence of a search having been made for it. The only related evidence I could find was in which police questioned Barry about a revolver seen in his possession soon after he left New Westminster. His answer appears in accounts of his trial.

The personal items bearing Charlie's name were mentioned in the report, bringing his identity into print for the first time, and dashing any wisp of hope Del Moses might have had that it was not his friend lying in the bush. The clothes, which had been suggested earlier as a possible key to identifying the body, were unremarkable. There was a black double-breasted vest, blue serge pants with drawers, a grey undershirt, a heavy grayish-brown over shirt, a small white neckerchief, and a pair of heavy nailed Wellingtons, size eight. A belt with a brass hook and eye was lying nearby. Why was it taken off the body? A likely explanation is suggested by a list of essential supplies for miners, published in *The Colonist* of January 16, 1898. The list mentions a type of money belt known as a "gold belt," so presumably the killer had checked to see if Charlie was wearing one. There was no sign of a hat, several types of which also made the list of essential supplies. Del Moses also reported that Charlie wore a wide-brimmed hat, but this was never found.

The coroner's jury returned a verdict of willful murder against some person or persons unknown, and before leaving the site Mr. Cox made arrangements to have the remains "decently interred."

Later, a search was made of the record of miners' licenses for the previous two years, but no trace of the name Blessing could be found. *The Sentinel* closed its report with the message: "We have thus been particular in describing the clothes, etc. as it is more than likely they may lead to the identity of the man; up to the present no one appears to know him."

Del Moses was probably the first to respond. He told his story to the authorities and soon after a warrant was sworn out for Barry's arrest. On Tuesday, October 2, one week after the initial report, Constable Sullivan set off in pursuit of the suspected killer.

Two days later *The Sentinel* got up to speed with a report headed "Further Particulars concerning the Murdered Man Blessing."

> From W.D. Moses, barber in this place, we gather the following particulars about the murdered man. It appears that when he was coming up here last spring he met Blessing at New Westminster, and becoming acquainted with him they traveled together as far as Quesnellemouth, which they reached on May 28; here Moses had business that detained him a few days, and Blessing feeling anxious to go on determined to start on the morning of May 30.
>
> On the evening previous to this departure, they got into a conversation with a man named James Barry, a perfect stranger to both, who said he was going up to Williams Creek next morning, and it was agreed that they should go together; they had several drinks at Brown & Gillis Saloon [the Occidental],

in paying for which Blessing changed a twenty-dollar bank note, remarking to Moses that he had a few more left and at the same time telling him that he did not like the looks of the stranger, he promised to meet Moses at Van Winkle, where he had some friends, since that night Moses has neither seen nor heard of the man.

While traveling together, he informed Moses that he had been mining on Lightning Creek [at Van Winkle] in 1862, but had returned the same year to California, and had lived at Calaveras County ever since; that he was an American by birth and belonged to some of the Eastern States; he also told him that his name was Charles Blessing; and observed at the time that as it was a very uncommon name he (Moses) would be very apt to remember it if anything were to happen to him.

Moses left Quesnellemouth and arrived at Van Winkle on the first of June, but could hear nothing of the man; about a week after he arrived in Williams Creek he met Barry and asked him what he had done to his "chummy" to which he replied that he had left him on the road and had not seen him since, Moses thought no more of the matter until he saw the name of the murdered man in *The Sentinel,* when the circumstances above related flashed across his memory at once, and he hurried to the magistrate and gave him the information.

This man Barry, on whom a very strong suspicion now rests as being the murderer, left the creek in great haste the day after the news arrived of the discovery of the body. It is said that he is well known as a bad character to the police of Victoria, where he kept a hurdy-gurdy dance house in Johnson Street last winter. In the early part of the summer he was arrested here on a charge of stealing a pair of gum boots, but has been discharged for want of evidence. Officer Sullivan has been dispatched after him, and will telegraph from Quesnellemouth to Yale to have him arrested should he reach there before he is overtaken.

The reference to Quesnellemouth in the last paragraph does not tie in with other accounts, which have Sullivan following Barry to Soda Creek along a fur trapper's trail, so is likely to have been an error based on an assumption made by the journalist. This is made even more likely by Sullivan's testimony at a preliminary hearing on the charge against Barry on October 16.

Sullivan told the court that he had pursued Barry to Soda Creek and that when he learned his quarry had headed further south on the stage, he telegraphed ahead from there to Yale and Lytton. No mention was made of Quesnellemouth.

Sullivan's telegrams were successful and Barry was arrested at Yale, in spite of giving a false name. Sullivan reached Yale on October 8 and took Barry into custody. Later the same day, they began their journey back to Barkerville. Sullivan said that Barry was generally well behaved and seemed ready to talk. Even when Sullivan warned him that anything he said could be taken down and used as evidence, he persisted, and in the course of their conversations he made several contradictory statements.

> When passing Cornwall's [a roadhouse] on the way up, the prisoner asked me who laid the charge against him," said Sullivan. "I told him he would find all that out when he arrived on the Creek He said to me he guessed he could tell me who it was. He said he was sure it was Moses, a coloured barber on Williams Creek, as Moses had asked two or three times what became of the man [Blessing] who came up the road with him." Barry said that Moses had asked so often he got vexed with him and said "What do I care about the man; I'm no caretaker of his.

When Sullivan repeated this at the hearing, *The Sentinel* reported that Barry, "in a rather excited state," called out "I said no such thing."

Barry also told Sullivan that he had enough money when he came on the Creek, but went through it on the Hurdies. Later in the journey, Sullivan reintroduced the topic of money, saying: "So you say, Barry, you had plenty of money when you came on the Creek and you went through it on the Hurdies?" Barry first denied the remark and then corrected himself. He had a little money, he said, but did not spend much of it on the Hurdies.

Sullivan and Barry reached the Creek on Sunday, October 14, and a record made in the Barkerville County Court Record Book, which served as a police charge book, states:

> James Berry [sic], given in custody by Constable J.H. Sullivan, charged on suspicion of the murder of C.M. Blessing. Personal property: None. Description: Height 5ft 6½in. and stout; hair brown. Age 29. Hair on face sandy and scant.

If he had no personal property, Barry must have left Barkerville traveling light, or else have disposed of it in Soda Creek, perhaps to raise money for the stage. Whatever the reason, he had to face his accusers, including Del Moses, in court just two days later. The hearing was held in the old Richfield Courthouse before Mr. Cox, now acting in his capacity as Police Magistrate. *The Sentinel* reported that proceedings began at 2:00 p.m. and that "the room in a few minutes was filled with a crowd of anxious spectators."

No one wanted to miss what would happen next.

• • •

1. I still have trouble with the "shot at." A grouse is a relatively small bird and unless it was hit with a shotgun loaded with birdshot there wouldn't have been much left to eat. If Guichon was carrying a gun for protection, it is unlikely to have been loaded with birdshot, so I favor other reports that he threw a stone at it. Chief among these is an account written for the *British Columbia Digest* by Lawrence P. Guichon, the son of the packer.

Chapter Five

Caught on the Wire

The day before the hearing, *The Sentinel* praised Constable Sullivan, saying:

> Great credit is due to the alacrity displayed by officer Sullivan, in procuring the arrest of the man James Barry who stands accused of the murder of C.M. Blessing near Beaver Pass & who arrived here yesterday in custody of Mr. Sullivan. It will be remembered that several days had elapsed after the accused left this place before Mr. Sullivan was dispatched on his tracks, arriving at Soda Creek he discovered the accused had taken the stage to Yale. Mr. Spalding[1] happening to be at Soda Creek on business, Mr. Sullivan asked him to telegraph to Mr. Sanders, at Yale, giving a description of the fugitive with orders for his arrest, and then proceeded down with the stage. Only 12 hours elapsed after the message reached Yale before the stage arrived there and the arrest was made…

Today, the street performers at Barkerville often pay tributes of their own to the policeman who covered more than 100 miles on horseback at such a speed that he nearly overhauled Barry at Soda Creek, in spite of the killer having a head start of nearly a week.

The first witness called at the hearing was another policeman, Chief Constable W.H. Fitzgerald, who accompanied Mr. Cox to the spot where Charlie's body was found. As his evidence was a reiteration of information published already about the finding of the body, *The Sentinel's* reporter passed on to the testimony of Constable Sullivan. This was substantially as presented in the previous chapter, but Sullivan also testified that during their journey back he had asked Barry why he had given the name "James Corbett" when first questioned at Yale. Barry's response was that he thought the constable was a newspaper reporter and that he just did it for a lark.

When Sullivan asked Barry what he had done with the pistol he had sometimes been seen wearing tucked into his belt, Barry said that he had first tried to sell it at the Creek but gave up when he was unable to get even $5 for it. Later, when he was tossing for drinks at Wallace's 13 Mile House, he lost and was forced to sell the pistol to Dutch Bill, the packer, to pay his debt. (Dutch Bill, or William Dietz, was the man after whom Williams Creek was named. His claim proved to be, ironically, among the poorest in what was one of the world's richest gold-bearing creeks.)

Sullivan said that, so far as he could determine, the name of the murdered man was not known in Yale at the time of Barry's arrest. In fact, the constable there had asked him if the dead man had been identified. If the identity of the man was unknown to the public at large, Barry made a serious tactical error by being so quick to accuse Del Moses of informing on him. There was only one way he could have known that the barber's friend was the dead man. Great importance would be attached to this type of slip-up when he came before Judge Begbie at the assizes a year later.

Perhaps Barry sensed that he had made a mistake, because, when asked if he had anything to say in response to Constable Sullivan's evidence, he said: "Sullivan is mistaken about what I told him concerning the man on our way up."[2]

Next in the stream of witnesses after Sullivan was Del Moses who told the story of how he and Blessing had traveled to Quesnellemouth and then parted company. He recalled Blessing's misgivings about going on with Barry, and mentioned how he had urged his friend to stay and travel with him instead. Moses said that on his last night in Quesnellemouth, Blessing had gone with Barry to doss down in an empty house belonging to Marks and Winkler. The next day, Moses called around there to see if they had left. They had.

In cross-examination, Barry asked him: "Are you sure that the man started with me from Quesnellemouth?"

"You told me so yourself," Moses replied.

"I never told you so."

There things would have remained — one man's word against another — if the police hadn't found another witness. His name was John Elliott and he said he knew the prisoner.

> On the morning of the 30th of May last I went into an old house belonging to Marks and Winkler at Quesnellemouth. I saw the prisoner and Blessing rolling up their blankets. I did not see them again until I got to Wallace's at the 13 Mile House. The prisoner and Blessing were sitting there. I stopped there for about an hour and went on, leaving them at Wallace's and did not see them again until the next morning, before breakfast time. They had passed Boyd and Heath's house. I saw them again between Boyd and Heath's and Edwards' [place]. They were camped on the right hand side of the road near a small stream…The next place I saw the prisoner was at Van Winkle. I asked him where his partner was. He told me he had sore feet and he left him behind. I saw [the] prisoner again on the Creek about [the] 2nd of June.

H.P. Stark, who traveled part of the way to Williams Creek with Elliott, said he had known Barry for about two years.

> I recollect seeing him on the 29th of May last at Quesnellemouth," he said. "I asked him when he was going to leave for the Creek…he said next morning. I left about six o'clock on the morning of the 30th in company with John

Elliot, the former witness. On coming to the 13 Mile House I saw the prisoner and another man sitting on a bench.

After [I had been] resting for three quarters of an hour, Mr. Gannon came along with some cattle. I asked Elliott to go on ahead of them [Stark didn't want to walk behind the mob of cattle]. Elliott, Barry, the other man, and I left the house together. Elliott and I soon distanced the other two as they walked slowly. Elliott and I got to Boyd's that night. I left next morning alone as Elliott stopped to help Gannon with his cattle.

Stark said he reached Van Winkle at about four in the afternoon and some two hours later, he saw Barry arrive without Blessing. Barry's being alone would not have seemed significant at the time as traveling companions came and went along the trail. Even Stark had left Elliott behind when the latter chose to earn a bit of extra money helping drive the cattle. It was only with hindsight that the absence of "the other man" became significant.

How sad that of all the witnesses who saw Barry on the trail, only Elliott seemed to know the name of his companion. Charlie was always "the other man." In the normal course of events, traveling companions would be expected to introduce each other, but it seems that Del Moses was correct in describing Charlie as a shy, almost timid man.

Barry, on the other hand, seemed to be known by many people. Among those giving evidence was William Fraser, a former workmate. Fraser said he had known Barry since April of the year before when they met whilst working at Moody's sawmill in New Westminster.

On May 14, 1866, he and Barry set off north together in the company of two other men: Daniel Fraser [no relation] and William Mann. The foursome would stay together all the way to Quesnellemouth and William Fraser had special cause to keep a close eye on Barry. He was particularly interested in a six-shooter that Barry was carrying. Fred Powers, the watchman at Moody's sawmill, had asked him to take a close look at the gun, because his had been stolen and he suspected that Barry was the culprit. Fraser saw Barry wearing a gun in his belt and managed to take a close look at it, but wasn't able to make out the serial number.

That gun wasn't the only odd thing about Barry.

"We stopped one night at Lytton and started [out] about seven or eight o'clock the next morning," said Fraser. "About a mile on this side [north] of Lytton we came to a gully full of rocks. James Barry remarked that there was $1,400 hid there alongside of a rock. He said it was in an oyster can."

Barry went off the trail to examine the spot more closely, but returned empty-handed.

"He said he would not mind it now for fear someone would haul him up for it," said Fraser. "I said 'Jamie, how did you find out there was money hid there?' He said a man who was in the chain gang at New Westminster told him so. He cautioned me to say nothing about it for fear he might be hauled up."

The foursome reached Quesnellemouth on or about the May 28. The next day, William Fraser said Barry asked him for some money to keep him until he got to the Creek. He refused. Barry then turned his attentions to Daniel Fraser who lent him $5.

William Fraser said that he and Daniel left Barry behind "at the 'Mouth," but on the morning they left, he noticed that Barry still had the pistol and had slept with it under his pillow. The next time he saw Barry was on June 1 at Cameronton. Barry was dancing with the Hurdies.

The Sentinel saw fit to record the testimony of two more witnesses — Messrs. S.J. Wilcox and H. Thompson.

"[The] prisoner came to my house on the 4th of June last in the evening and asked the price of board," said Wilcox. "I told him $12 a week in advance. He asked if it was customary to pay in advance. I told him it was when the parties were strangers to me. He threw down a $20 gold piece and I gave him the change. He paid the next week $10 in advance with a $10 Bank of British Columbia note. The third week he paid $10 in advance. After this, Mr. Washburn became responsible for his board as he worked for him."

Wilcox said Barry wore a revolver slung in his belt, and at their first meeting said it had been of good service to him in the army.

Thompson reported that he had met Barry in the spring of 1865 when he was working for a Mr. Lewis in New Westminster. However, he did not see him again until June 10, 1866 in Barkerville.

"He came down to the tunnel in which I was working in Mr. Arthur's gulch and said he had been to Edwards' since he had seen me last. I asked him what took him there. He said he went out after some clothes he left there on his way up. He was doing nothing and thought he might as well go after the clothes as buy new ones."

At the end of the hearing the charge was read over to Barry and he was asked, "after receiving the usual admonition from the magistrate," if he had anything to say.

The Sentinel wrote: "The prisoner replied in an agitated tone of voice that he had nothing [to say] except that he was innocent of the charge."

The impression one gains of Barry is that he was a cocky fellow, somewhat prone to "big noting" or posturing. There was that business with the $1,400 on the trail, for example. If he was on the level about it and so broke that he needed to ask his companions for loans, he would have taken something from the oyster tin to tide him over — if it had existed. Instead, it appears he was trying to play the tough guy who was privy to the confidences of men on the chain gang. He had a need to feel important and enjoyed being the centre of attention. He wasn't imposing physically, so perhaps he tried to make himself bigger in other ways.

There is nothing to be found to substantiate his claim to being in "the army," but a reference to him said that although he was usually regarded as a Texan, he hailed originally from Sligo in Ireland. The same source said he was good with horses.

The gun in Barry's belt was part of his swagger, and so too was his rude and arrogant behavior in throwing down a twenty-dollar gold piece in front of Wilcox. "You want money? Of course I've got money! And there's plenty more where this came from!" When he got to the Creek, Barry spent time with the Hurdies. There's nothing unusual in that. After all, they were some of the few unattached women in a predominantly male society, and many of the miners must have bought time with them. However, Barry initially told Sullivan that he had not just had a dance or two with them, but had gone through his money on the Hurdies. He backtracked later, of course, but that was after he realized where Sullivan's questions about money were leading.

In any event, Mr. Cox committed him to appear at the next assizes and bound over the witnesses on their own recognizance in the sum of £100[3] each to appear at the trial. However, it would be a year before Barry was brought before Judge Begbie, a year in which the prosecutors scrambled about trying to find more witnesses and persuade them to stay put, and a year in which Barry could work out a more convincing story.

In the meantime, Moses started a collection in the community to buy a wooden grave marker for Blessing. Once erected, it displayed a simple inscription:

> In memory of C.M. Blessing, native of Ohio, aged 30 years.
> Was murdered near this spot, May 31, 1866.

All Moses wanted to do was to honor Charlie's plea to be remembered. He had no way of knowing that this simple gesture from one friend to another would give flower more than 100 years later to British Columbia's smallest historic park.

• • •

1. A telegraph company official. Other reports indicate that the line had been installed and was being tested before going into service. This early use by Constable Sullivan is believed to be the first time the telegraph was employed in an arrest in what is now the Province of British Columbia. Without it, Barry is likely to have made good his escape.
2. This response seems stilted — an effect that probably owes more to *The Sentinel* reporter's paraphrasing than what Barry actually said. I have resisted temptations to "polish" such statements for fear of changing the meaning of the original testimony. Bear in mind that when this book was written, I was drawing from material already more than 135 years old.
3. Approximately $1,200 US in nominal value, but the actual buying power could have been as high as $9,220, according to an online historical cash converter I tried.

Chapter Six

"The Most Sordid of Motives"

The session of the Richfield Assizes that opened on July 4, 1867 had three cases to consider, two of which would become the first in the district to involve sentences of death. Barry was being tried for the murder of Blessing; a native Indian named Nikel Palsk was accused of murdering another prospector named John Morgan; and a Williams Creek character, Hard Curry, faced a charge of perjury.

Incidentally, the surname of Palsk's victim has caused some people to become confused between him and Charlie. I have even seen newspaper articles referring to Barry's victim as "Morgan." The man who wanted to be remembered had lost a third of his name. And while on the subject, another article said Palsk was Chinese. One reporter got Del's name wrong twice, referring to him first as "James Wëllington Moses" and then "James Washington Moses." James Barry is sometimes called "Jack" or "John," and his surname was even reported as "Berry," which probably means the reporter was influenced by the boo-boo in the 1866 police charge book.

Although a good argument can be made that the extreme levels of violence in the Barry and Palsk cases were out of character for the relatively law-abiding Cariboo, this doesn't mean that the miners were a pack of choir boys. They encountered violence everywhere — at work, at play, and even the environment acted against them at times.

Consider, for example, various news stories covered in a single page of *The Sentinel.* There is a report of a cave-in that buried two men trying to shore up a drift at Grouse Creek. The foreman dug one of the men out, relatively unharmed, but the other died soon after from a broken back.

A prizefight is reported in which Ned Stein defeated the 4:1 favorite, Johnny Knott, in *forty-nine* rounds. Plenty of blood and gore was evidenced there, no doubt.

There is a report of a spluttering bomb being found near the tents of the Volunteer Camp. When a sentry noticed the bomb, a voice called out of the darkness, "Mind, it will explode." The sentry picked up the bomb and threw it in the direction of the voice. Fortunately, the wick fell out. *The Sentinel* reported that the bomb was made from a soda bottle three-quarters filled with blasting powder, topped off with sawdust and ground glass. The bomb was considered "very similar to what is used sometimes in parts of the old country for damaging machinery when hands are on strike."

A further article about a violent killing, titled "The Would Be Murderer Killed," relates to an oblique attempt Barry would later make to implicate "Chinamen" in the killing of Charlie. Perhaps he thought reports such as this would lend credibility to his argument. In any event, this incident happened at Wallace's 13 Mile House, the place where Barry said he had lost his six-shooter while tossing for drinks. It was also where John Elliott remembered noticing Barry with Blessing, and Stark noticed "the other man." It was, therefore, one of the last places Charlie was seen alive.

The first act in what *The Sentinel* called "a singular and bloody tragedy" opened around noon on Saturday, August 4, 1866, when Alexander Wallace served two Chinese men some coffee and refreshments. One of the men paid him and they left without incident or any comments. Some fifteen minutes later, one of the men returned. Wallace was stooped over, fixing up some boards behind the bar. The man picked up a hatchet and leaned over the bar, striking Wallace a fierce blow on the head that removed about three square inches of scalp and slightly fractured his skull. Wallace had barely recovered from the shock when the man made an attempt to hit him again. However, he had to lean so far forward that his arm struck the bar on the way down and sent the hatchet spinning from his hand.

Wallace rushed his assailant, who drew a knife. The two struggled and Wallace managed to wrest control of the knife. They grappled with each other, stumbled outside and fell to the ground where Wallace used the knife on his attacker, striking several blows, which *The Sentinel* reported, "deprived the despicable wretch of existence."

Fearing that the dead man's former companion might be in the neighborhood, Wallace hastened off to Quesnellemouth to turn himself in to the police. About a mile from his house, he met Alex Burnett, a packer, who later described Wallace as being in a weak state. Burnett listened to Wallace's story, gave him a mule to ease his journey to Quesnellemouth, and then set off for 13 Mile House to investigate. He found the Chinese man lying dead outside the door of the house, with large wounds in his neck, side, and chest.

On his way back toward Quesnellemouth, Burnett overtook another Chinese man whom he presumed to have been the second of Wallace's customers. He "took him in charge," according to *The Sentinel,* and delivered him to the authorities. No reference is made as to whether Wallace also saw this man on the road.

The Chinese man told police that he was in service to Kwong Lee & Co. and had come from Williams Creek where he had been collecting money for his employers. He had met the other man outside 13 Mile House and they had gone in together for something to eat. He paid their bill and they left together. Outside, they chatted for a while, during which time the other man remarked that Wallace appeared to have plenty of money.

Soon after, they said their farewells and went their separate ways, the witness heading for Quesnellemouth and the other man for Williams Creek. As there was no evidence to implicate him in the attack, the witness was discharged.

The dead man was said to have been "a large, powerful fellow"

Barkerville Outlived its Newspaper

The Cariboo Sentinel, the newspaper that told the story of the murder of Charles Morgan Blessing, and declared that Barkerville was "here to stay" was outlived by the town it served.

Day One for *The Sentinel* was June 6, 1865 and, in spite of its great confidence in the future of the town once billed as the largest west of Chicago and north of San Francisco, the final edition came off the press some ten years later.

When it began, *The Sentinel* was first published weekly, but switched to bi-weekly in October 1965. The proprietor, George Wallace, sold his interest to Allan Lambert who had worked on *The Victoria Colonist.* After a short period, Lambert sold out to Robert Holloway who stayed with the paper until the end. When Lambert moved south, he started *The Yale Tribune.*

The press used by *The Sentinel* had its own place in history, being used to print the first newspaper in what is now British Columbia. This was the French language *Le Courier de la Nouvelle Caledonie.* Later still, the same press turned out the first issues of *The Victoria Colonist.*

about five feet, eleven inches tall. He was reported to be a gambler who had lost all his money in Quesnellemouth and was on his way to Williams Creek "dead broke."

All of these stories came from one page of a newspaper that served what was said to be a relatively law-abiding district! This also represented the world into which Charlie Blessing and Del Moses had ventured. By Californian standards it might have been law abiding, but life was still hard and tough.

When Judge Begbie took his place at the bench of Richfield Courthouse around 10:00 a.m. on July 4, 1867, he was accompanied by His Honor H.M. Hall, Mr. C.E. Pooley (the Registrar) and Deputy Sheriff F.V. Lee.

The first task was to swear in a grand jury. Those empanelled were: J.H. Todd (foreman), M. Winkler, D. Oppenheimer, E.A. Wadhams, Dr. Wilkinson, L. Twing, R.R. Monro, John Polmere, John Work, E. Dewdney, F. Neufelder, J.J. Bramley, H.S. Blunt, J.O. Floyd, Dr. Carrall, A. Huffmeister, John Adair, C. Strouss, T. Buie, and I. Weill.

Judge Begbie spoke to them of "the unusual number of the cases and the enormity of the offences charged" and adjourned the court to deliberate on the indictments presented. After an hour, true bills[1] were brought in against each of the three men facing charges. When Judge Begbie returned to the bench, Barry was brought before him and the indictment read over to him. He entered a plea of not guilty.

The following were then empanelled as a jury: W. Winnard (foreman), George Wilson, E. Vaughn, C.A. Brouse, William Langen, E. Pearson, C. Moorhouse, James Mann, A. Clink, George Dakin, Frank Lecuyer, and W.S. Melross.

The prosecutor was Mr. H.P. Walker and Barry was defended by Mr. A.R. Robertson.[2]

The Sentinel reported that Mr. Walker opened the case against Barry with "a speech of considerable length." The reporter quoted none of it, but said simply that Walker "recited the various circumstances connected with the murder that he was prepared to bring evidence to establish."

As in the preliminary hearing, the first witness called was Chief Constable Fitzgerald who essentially recapped his earlier statements about the finding of the body and the various personal effects. However, he brought new evidence in the form of two gold pins that have since added much to the folklore surrounding Charlie's death. Judge Begbie took a close look at them and even sketched them in the margin of his bench book.

"I took them from a dancing girl last autumn," said Fitzgerald, "and they have been in my hands ever since. One remarkable feature about one of them is that when turned in a certain way, the profile of a man's face is distinctly shown."

Some more sensational accounts of Blessing's story later said that the nugget was shaped like an angel with wings outstretched. This allowed them to speak of "the guardian angel" playing a part in bringing Barry to justice. However, Judge Begbie's sketch shows a man's head only, and to see it at all the pin has to be turned upside down. His sketch of the second nugget shows a simple blob of gold fastened to the head of the pin. The judge drew a small chain dangling from this pin.

During cross-examination by Robertson, Fitzgerald said the

"head" pin was so distinctive he would recognize it years after having seen it. He also said that the body was found fifty yards from the Wagon Road and within twenty feet of the old trail.

"My impression is that the murder was committed on the trail, as the ground is steep toward the road" he said.

In response to another question from Mr. Robertson, Fitzgerald agreed that it was possible that he might have overlooked paper money sewn into Blessing's clothes — a common practice by travelers at the time. There was also the possibility that paper money might have disintegrated after four months in the outdoors.

Changing Times

The Occidental Hotel in Quesnellemouth, where Charles Morgan Blessing made his fatal decision to travel on to the goldfields with James Barry, once did some traveling of its own. When Front Street was developed, the hotel was moved back from its original riverbank location to make room for the roadway.

But that was not all that changed. The hotel was built to serve the burgeoning town of Quesnellemouth, which was to shorten its name to Quesnel. The hotel followed suit and became the Quesnel Hotel.

The proprietors at the time that Charlie Blessing and Del Moses passed through were Thomas Brown and Hugh Gillis, hence the popular name for the hotel, "Brown and Gillis's."

Gillis committed suicide in 1871, leaving Brown as the sole proprietor. When he died ten years later, the operation of the hotel was left to his widow, Sarah Ann, and the manager John McLean. They later married, and retired in 1900.

The town was named Quesnellemouth in honor of Jules Maurice Quesnelle, a member of Simon Fraser's company that made the epic first journey down what would become known as the Fraser River. The town still thrives at the junction of the Fraser and Quesnel Rivers.

Over time the name was shortened to Quesnelmouth and then Quesnel. One of the reasons for this was probably sheer convenience. For example, the newspapers of the day used type that was handset, letter by letter. Any shortcuts that would save time and effort were welcomed. Quesnelmouth could be set more quickly than Quesnellemouth and Quesnel much faster than both.

Del Moses was the next witness, and also largely repeated his evidence from the preliminary hearing. It is important to note that, in spite of many popular accounts given in the 1900s, he made no mention of the gold pins at either appearance. He also made no mention of Barry coming into the barbershop wearing the pin — another popular fable. Neither did he mention the ghost of Blessing coming in for a shave, yet another lurid tale that has had its time in print.

Moses did mention that at Quesnellemouth Blessing told him he was not broke yet and had $50–60 left. Today that might not seem worth killing a man for, but then it was more than some workers got in a month. Also, Barry might have expected Charlie to be carrying more. In cross-examination, Moses said that Barry was standing close enough to them in the bar at Quesnellemouth to overhear the conversation about money, but he couldn't say whether he had for sure. All the money Moses had seen Blessing with was $20 at the Junction and one banknote at Quesnellemouth.

Up to this point it seemed certain that Barry was guilty. Then Moses made a comment that started to raise the first few wisps of doubt.

"We came up by steamer from Soda Creek because Blessing had a slight gall [a sore caused by friction and abrasion] on his heel from his boot," he said. Blessing did have a sore foot and was said to have been walking slowly when he was with Barry. What else about Barry's story might be true? Could someone else have killed Charlie after Barry had left him alone at trailside?

In answer to another question, Moses said he couldn't remember whether Charlie had put his name on any of his possessions, but he said the items found near the body looked like ones Charlie owned.

Speaking of the morning he had gone early to see if Barry and Blessing had left the house where they had spent the night, Moses said there had been very heavy rain and that he thought of them both having to travel through it at the time. Judge Begbie might have nodded in sympathy because he wrote in his bench book "atrocious weather."

How much would heavy rain and muddy footing have aggravated the sore on Charlie's foot? The glimmer of doubt persists.

Were similar thoughts going through Judge Begbie's mind? Was Barry's lawyer scoring points here?

Moses continued his testimony, telling once again how he had asked fruitlessly after Charlie at Macaffery's in Van Winkle, and his decision to carry on to Williams Creek alone. He had reached Barkerville on June 1 and gone looking for somewhere to set up shop.

"A day or two after this, Barry came into my shop and I enquired of him where my Chummy was. He said, 'Your Chummy, who is he?' I said the man who left Quesnellemouth with you. He replied, 'That coon...I left him on the road...his feet were sore.' I asked him what time they left [Quesnellemouth] that morning, and he said about four or five o'clock.

"On a second occasion I asked Barry about Blessing, and got the same answer. Some time afterwards I asked him a third time if he had seen the man yet...he looked savagely at me, and muttered something I could not understand, but seeing he did not like it I asked no more."

In cross-examination, Moses said he couldn't remember who had spoken to whom first in the barbershop.

H.P. Stark repeated his evidence from the preliminary hearing as well, but John Elliott apparently did not testify. Perhaps he had risked his $100 bond and left the district? Prospectors were always moving on in search of greener — or in this case, more golden — pastures. Stark did add though that soon after seeing Barry arrive in Van Winkle he had heard Elliott ask him about the man who had been traveling with him. Barry had replied that the man had got sore feet and stayed behind at Beaver Pass.

Stark said he knew of no one else who saw Barry that night and couldn't remember what time it was when he and Elliott had seen him. When asked if he knew where Elliott was, Stark said he had seen him "going down country last January to get work at the 13 Mile House."

During cross-examination, Stark said that he could not describe the prisoner's companion. The next part of Begbie's notes has an indistinct word that could be "lame." If so, Stark might then have said of Barry's companion: "He looked to walk lame at the 13 Mile House."

Stark said there were several Chinamen at work about the road and he also saw other white men. Asked about the traveling conditions, he said that the roads were in good order, but very muddy. However, he did not take the trail cut-off used by Barry and his companion.

Patrick Gannon, the cattle drover Elliott had helped out, said that the previous summer, when he was bringing cattle to the Creek, he had seen Barry taking breakfast with another man at a campfire on the Barkerville side of Boyd and Heaths.

"I got off [my horse] to light a pipe, but I was in a hurry and didn't take much notice of the other man."

Gannon continued on to Williams Creek, but camped en route at Van Winkle where he saw Barry at around 6:00 or 7:00 p.m. He heard Elliott ask Barry where he had left his comrade. Barry said the man had sore feet so he left him behind.

Suddenly, Barry's reason for leaving Charlie behind is gaining credence.

William Fraser and Constable Sullivan both added new material to their earlier evidence. Sullivan reported that during their trip back from Yale, Barry had told him he left Quesnellemouth alone, but overtook a Frenchman on the way. Fraser said that Barry still had the six-shooter at Quesnellemouth and implied that the prisoner was trigger-happy.

"On one occasion," he said, "Barry wanted to shoot into a crowd and I said 'no.'"

Just before he left Quesnellemouth, Barry had asked if he could borrow $5. Fraser refused. He had already had to settle Barry's bar tab. Barry then went to Daniel Fraser and borrowed the $5 mentioned at the preliminary hearing.

William Fraser said that he later saw Barry at Cameronton dancing with the Hurdies, and on several occasions saw him pay cash. Like Barry, he was then boarding with Mr. Wilcox.

In cross-examination, Fraser conceded that Barry might have found work, but said, "I don't think he had work when he got on the Creek. I don't think he had any anyway. He told me he had none. He worked only a little at New Westminster."

George Gartley was one of several new witnesses found in the year between the preliminary hearing and the trial. He said he'd traveled with Blessing by steamer from San Francisco the previous spring and had seen Blessing with two gold specimen pins which he thought had been connected by a small chain. Gartley said Blessing valued the specimen pins greatly because he had dug the nuggets out of the mines by himself.

"He showed me this pin," said Gartley, indicating one of the exhibits. "He said the jeweler had put it in upside down. I can swear to it. He asked me first to look at the pin and examine it and then asked if I could see anything particular. He then turned it upside down [to reveal the head shape]."

In cross-examination, he said that while Blessing showed him the pin once only, he was sure it was the same as the pin exhibited.

"I have seen many specimens, but none like the one produced."

William Love, another new witness, gave evidence that corroborated Gartley's testimony as to the uniqueness of the pin.

"He asked us if we could see anything particular. We said 'no.' He then reversed it and we saw the man's face."

Love told Mr. Robertson that while he did not know Blessing by name, he heard people calling him by that name. Like Gartley, he was shown the pin once only.

Next came Frederick Dibble who said he had worked with Barry the previous summer.

"We had a conversation about the Hurdies with whom he had been dancing," Dibble said. "He showed me two pins — one of which I now identify — and said that they [the Hurdies] wanted them. He had been dancing with the Hurdies."

Dibble said he could remember that there was supposed to be something peculiar about one of the pins, but he couldn't recollect what it was.

"I said they looked like California gold and asked where he got them. He gave no satisfactory answer."

In cross-examination, Dibble said he saw the special pin only once, but got to hold it in his palm.

Thomas A. Barry, who with N. Cunio had purchased the Fashion Saloon in Barkerville the previous year, reported that he had seen the prisoner often (Judge Begbie refers to the saloon as a "dancing establishment" in his notes).

"He frequently came into the house and has danced for a dollar a dance. He always paid me when he danced."

Under cross-examination he said the prisoner was working "a great portion of the time" and always behaved well "as far as I saw…He has been in the house without dancing…He has danced sometimes without paying at the time…He has owed sometimes as much as $4 or $5."

The proprietor said he did not trust strangers, and that he did not know the prisoner before 1866.

As the prosecution kept questioning whether Barry had money of his own, the defense produced two witnesses in an attempt to prove that Barry had worked for his dancing money. George Baker said he thought the prisoner was working for him in June of 1866.

"He was working for me shortly after he came to the Creek for $7 per day. He was also working in the sawmills."

Baker said he could not be sure when he made payments to Barry.

"It might have been in July or August. Before he came to me he was working for Mr. Coombs, but I can't say exactly when."

Lorenzo K. Coombs said the prisoner worked for him for a few days in the early part of July, but added, "I am not positive as to the days."

Added to these would have to be the "Mr. Washburn" mentioned by Wilcox, the witness who had the twenty-dollar gold piece tossed down in front of him. At the preliminary hearing, Wilcox said Barry had paid for board from his own pocket until "Mr. Washburn became responsible for his board as he worked for him."

In spite of this evidence, it was clear from his bench notes that Judge Begbie was not overly impressed with Barry's work record.

In his summing up for the jury, Judge Begbie listed what he considered were the chief points at issue in the case. The bare outline of his remarks exists in his bench book, but it is not necessarily easy to read. In fact, the good judge's handwriting is at times almost indecipherable. Some sections were obviously written at speed as he scrambled to record testimony, often using his own abbreviations and short cuts. Sometimes words are reduced to initials letters followed by almost straight lines. (This is similar to a journalist's notes where key facts and figures are recorded along with sufficient words and phrases to trigger a good reconstruction.

It was more important to listen carefully to and understand what was being said than it was to record every golden word.)

Judge Begbie's starting point was the obvious question, "Was there a murder"? He wrote this across the top of the page. The coroner's investigation had answered this already — that bullet hole in the back of the head. Next came the equally obvious follow-up: "Who was the murderer?" Below this Judge Begbie listed seven points that he considered when answering the second question. These were:

1) WHO WAS LAST WITH HIM (THE VICTIM)? The prisoner and the victim agreed to go together from Quesnellemouth. They started out together between 3:00 and 4:00 a.m. They were seen together twice. Then there is what appears to be the word "admitted," which would make the next section read, "admitted over and over again." Finally, come four terse words: "corpse found en route."

2) MOTIVE? The deceased had $50–60. The prisoner was "utterly broken"…borrowed all the way up and at Quesnellemouth. Nothing traceable taken, only money — except gold pins.

3) PROPERTY FOUND. Gold pins in Blessing's possession in May; in June or July with prisoner in treating with a Hurdy. In November with a Hurdy. Prisoner had money generally and no work for wages until July.

4) PREVIOUS CHARACTER. Confidential communications with a man in the chain gang.

5) CHARACTER OF DECEASED. Very timid.

6) IDENTITY OF DECEASED. Surely beyond a doubt. Same height, hair, necktie. Various articles. Same locality in which Blessing disappeared.

7) SUBSEQUENT CONDUCT OF PRISONER. Immediate attempt to escape and giving false name.

These then were seen as the most important questions in deciding Barry's guilt. Barry and Blessing agreed to travel together, and they were seen together en route by several witnesses. Barry was broke and Blessing had money. The body was found near where Blessing was last seen. There was no money found on the body, although various items of clothing and personal effects indicated that it was Blessing. Barry appeared to have money when he arrived at the Creek and no conclusive proof was advanced that he had worked until July. He had even told the witness H. Thompson on June 10 that as he had nothing doing he might as well go back for the clothes he had left behind en route to the Creek. And then came Barry's flight as soon as he learned that a body had been found. This and his giving of a false name at Yale seemed to be points that Judge Begbie took as some of the strongest indicators of guilt.

So too did the jury. The twelve good men and true retired for only an hour before returning a verdict of guilty. Judge Begbie adjourned the case until the next day for sentencing, and as his gavel descended it could well have sounded to Barry like the first blow of the hammers that would soon be used in erecting his scaffold.

• • •

1. A bill of indictment issued after a *prima facie* case has been established.
2. A little more than a year earlier, Mr. Robertson had offered a thirty-dollar reward in *The Sentinel* to anyone who returned a box of law books and papers, addressed to him, which went missing somewhere between the 127 and 150 mile posts. He asked them to return the box to any Barnard's Express man. His advertisement, not far from one placed by Del Moses for his hair invigorator, evokes a comical picture of the box flying off the roof of the stage when it hit a bump in the road.

Chapter 7

Spinning Into Eternity

The cells at Richfield were attached to the court building and Barry would have been taken there overnight. It was by that time too late to hear Palsk's trial in the same day; one report from the park board files at Barkerville says it was 7:00 p.m. by the time the jury delivered its verdict against Barry.

He was still in the cells at 10:00 a.m. the next morning, Tuesday July 2, when the court convened to arraign the Indian for the murder of prospector John Morgan. There is evidence from newspaper reports that Palsk required an interpreter, Mr. K. Dewdney being sworn in for that task.

Notwithstanding this, the trial proceeded swiftly. Mr. H.P. Walker again acted as prosecutor and at the request of the judge Mr. G.A. Walkem represented Palsk.

The essential facts were that prospector Morgan was found dead near Soda Creek on November 7, 1865. The body was lying about 190 yards from the 172-mile post and about 60 yards from the Wagon Road. Constable Sullivan was called to the scene and conducted a preliminary examination. He noticed that the head had been crushed in and that there was a cut on one ear "running through to the skull." The next day he conducted a more careful investigation after Morgan's remains had been moved to a cabin. He found a gunshot wound on each side of the torso.

Sullivan said there were no valuables on the body and there was evidence of a watch having been cut from a leather watch guard. The missing watch was later recovered from a Mrs. Ritchie of Canoe Creek who said she had bought it from an Indian. A watchmaker named either F. or E. Hodgens (print indistinct in *The Sentinel*) identified the watch as having belonged to Morgan.

The most telling evidence came from Chil-Pecken, described in court as an accomplice of Palsk, who gave Queen's Evidence through the interpreter.

He said Palsk got a musket and a bottle of liquor at Quesnellemouth and they both went down the river and slept at a "siwash house¹" that night. The next morning they set off downriver again, taking a hatchet from the house. They came to where a white man was sitting eating and Palsk told Chil-Pecken that he would kill the man. Chil-Pecken asked him not to, so they continued on their way. Later they encountered the same man again. This time, Chil-Pecken offered him some whisky, but he declined. Palsk pointed his gun at the man and Chil-Pecken became afraid and backed off.

Palsk mocked him, saying, "What are you afraid of?" and fired the musket, hitting the man in the back. The wounded man grabbed his blankets and ran off. Palsk reloaded and they followed the man. Palsk fired again and the man fell.

"The prisoner told me to kill him with the small axe and I did so," said Chil-Pecken. "We hauled the body a short distance off...We took a $10 note, a gold watch, and a specimen [gold nugget] from the body...We both went to Mrs. Ritchie's at Canoe Creek and the prisoner sold the watch to her for $5.50 and the specimen for $2.50."

In cross-examination, Chil-Pecken told the court that the first shot had hit Morgan in the back and the second in the breast. He told Mr. Walkem that he had not been promised his liberty if he gave evidence against Palsk. In other words, he had not been bribed to say what the prosecutor wanted him to say in return for his freedom.

Chief Constable Fitzgerald said that when he arrested Palsk, the prisoner told him that he had bought the watch from an Indian and the specimen from a Spaniard. Palsk admitted selling both items to Mrs. Ritchie.

The jury retired to consider the evidence and returned only fifteen minutes later with a verdict of guilty.

At this point Barry was brought into the courtroom and both accused soon stood before Mr. Begbie for sentencing. Imagine them standing there, side by side. Two men from different backgrounds united in this moment before a judge already known for his uncompromising stand against villainy.

There is nothing in Judge Begbie's notes or *The Sentinel* reporter's account that describes their attitude at the time, although Barry is elsewhere described as cocky and Palsk as belligerent. These were the men described by *The Sentinel's* editorial writer respectively as a black-hearted villain and an unenlightened savage. Barry's earlier showing might have been mere bravado and an attempt to save face, but surely he would have realized by now that he was a walking dead man. How much did Palsk understand, though? Part of Mr. Walkem's task would have been to explain to him the significance of the jury's deliberations, but did he really understand that his life was on the line? Could he comprehend that these strange, soft, white men were preparing to take him outside and kill him, not in a fit of passion, but in cold blood — and possibly even with regret?

Perhaps Judge Begbie studied them both for a moment as he marshaled his thoughts before pronouncing sentence. Perhaps the men shifted their feet awkwardly under his scrutiny. Maybe Barry still maintained some swagger and stared back boldly. And what of the others in the courtroom…how did they feel? The place was packed, we know that much from *The Sentinel.* Was Del Moses there to see justice done for his Chummy? There is no indication in the reports that any of the witnesses were still there, but I like to think that somewhere, perhaps pushed into a corner, the barber was waiting to see justice done. This was a tableau moment, but seconds can stretch out for just so long before movement is restored.

Imagine Judge Begbie stirring and leaning forward slightly to ask Palsk if he had anything to say why sentence should not be passed upon him. Palsk's reply was a simple "no."

The judge would then have turned his attention to Barry, who replied that he had nothing more to say other than that he had not committed the murder.

When asked for a statement, Barry said, "I never remember traveling with any stranger until I got to the 13 Mile House. The stranger overtook me there. The witness, Stark, came up afterwards...we started out together. Stark and his companion went on. I traveled three quarters of a mile with the stranger and then parted from him and have not seen him since. I admit that Gannon saw me alongside of a campfire, but when I got there I found two men there; and after resting a little, I went off. I passed three or four Chinamen on the road and came to Van Winkle that night. This is all the statement I have to make."

This was the awful moment then — the sentencing. For this we can turn to *The Sentinel* report, which concentrates on what Judge Begbie said to Barry "who still maintained the same stolid indifference which he manifested throughout the whole trial."

"I concur with the verdict of the jury," said the judge. "It is one given after due consideration of the whole circumstances. It is a matter of extreme importance to have to decide on a matter of life and death." Again the steely stare — and perhaps a pause — before he delivered the next, ominous line. "The longer the jury considered the evidence, the more thoroughly were they convinced of your guilt."

Judge Begbie then began a careful and chilling recitation of what look like facts listed in answer to the seven-point checklist in his bench notes. Each one thumped home with the finality of a coffin nail.

- It is clear that you started with the murdered man from Quesnellemouth;
- That you knew he had money;
- That you were penniless;
- That you were seen at the 13 Mile House in his company, and again seen with him a short distance from the spot where the body was found;

- That the man was never more seen alive;
- You had money when you came on the Creek;
- You were in possession of a nugget belonging to the murdered man, which you disposed of to a witness which [or "who"] has not been produced;
- You are found in possession of a weapon that would produce the crime.
- I can no more doubt your guilt than if I had been an eyewitness to it. I have no doubt you seduced your victim to leave the road and then perpetrated the crime; and that you did it for booty, the most sordid of all motives; that you revelled [sic] for months on the proceeds and then left; that you gave a false name when apprehended.

You have given no explanation regarding the nugget and none as to the disappearance of Blessing; you have appeared perfectly indifferent. It has been proved that you did not work or do anything to get money. It is impossible to conceive a crime more wanton or more [indistinct passage] than that which has been committed. I can offer you no hope of mercy.

Judge Begbie suddenly widened his address to include both defendants.

Beside you stands a man with no common tie of blood or color, who slew a man, actuated with the like pernicious avarice; the same fate that dogged your footsteps awaits him. You have both dyed your hands in blood and must both suffer the same fate. The law for the savage as well as the Christian is death for death. My painful duty now is to pass the last sentence of the law upon you both, which is that you be taken to the place whence you came and from thence to the place of execution, there to be hanged by the neck until you are dead. And may the Lord have mercy on your souls.

The Sentinel reporter observed, "neither of the prisoners seemed in the least affected by the awful sentence pronounced. On the contrary, Barry seemed to make light of his position, to judge from his expression to the crowd assembled around the rear of the court house when he told them to 'clear the ranks' and let him pass."

And what of Hard Curry, the third man called to answer charges before Judge Begbie? His case was scheduled for the next morning and he was a no-show, leaving an embarrassed bondsman to face the judge. Two other bondsmen linked to the accused did not show either.

"I want the body of Hard Curry," demanded Judge Begbie. "This man was safe in the hands of the jailor *[sic]* but afterwards committed to your custody where he is still supposed to remain. You are responsible for him."

"I do not know where Hard Curry is," Mr. Parsons replied. "He went out prospecting some time ago and I have not seen him since."

Judge Begbie was undeterred. "If it should ever appear that you were cognizant of his disappearance, you will be liable to be indicted for his offence and subject to his punishment, which I may tell you would be seven years in the chain gang."

Hard Curry, who had been indicted for perjury, was declared an outlaw. Faced with the wrath of the fearsome judge, perhaps he is running still.

Barry and Palsk spent the best part of a month in their cells awaiting the arrival of the warrants for their execution. During this time Barry became quite ill, whether from infection or strain, as the community grew vociferous in protesting the delay. Now that the two had been found guilty, the citizens of Barkerville wanted the last chapter played out.

Remember that line from the editorial in *The Sentinel:* "We trust that no over-refined sentimentality will be allowed to interfere with what to us appears to be the Divine will." That just about sums up the way people felt in Barkerville as days passed with no clear word about the execution. There had been a crime and they had found a suspect. The suspect had been convicted and had sentence passed on him even though the process took nearly a year to complete. Now all they wanted was to finish it.

Certainly Moses had no trouble raising money for Charlie's headstone, and on the day of the executions *The Sentinel* reports a large crowd gathering at 5:00 a.m.

After reviewing the evidence presented in court it seems certain that Barry was guilty of Blessing's murder. However, was the investigation as thorough as it could have been? An RCMP officer agreed that more would have been done today; however, he rated the police effort as good for the times and circumstances. It must have been extremely difficult, first, to find witnesses and, second, to get them to stick around long enough to give evidence.

For Barry, in spite of his attempt at indifference, the post-sentencing period must have been terrible as the clock ticked down on the last moments of his life. The tempo would have increased when word reached him that the warrants had arrived and a date been set for Friday, August 8, 1866. It seems possible that he could have become ill from the stress alone. In spite of this though, he never confessed publicly to the crime. There was no expression of sympathy for Blessing either. Was it possible that Barry was in effect saying, "I didn't do it, so how can I feel sorry for something I didn't do?"

How hard it must have been to sleep through the night of August 7. Besides the discomfort of the fetters on his wrists, Barry would have been able to hear the hammers and rasping saws of the carpenters building his scaffold just a few yards from his cell. Like the *tock-tock-tock* of a ghastly metronome, each hammer blow brought him another few seconds closer to the end of his life.

The Sentinel reports that the spectacle of the district's first publication execution drew a large crowd to the vicinity of the courthouse even before the scaffold had been completed. This means that Barry and Palsk would have been able to hear the murmur of voices outside as people waited to see them die.

At about 5:30 a.m. the sheriff and his posse came to the prisoners' cells and told them that their last moments had arrived. As the chains came off, the only remark Barry made was that he hoped no one else present would ever be placed in his awful position. Other than that, he remained calm.

Not so Palsk. The moment his shackles were removed, the Indian started to shout and struggle. The rather pompous account in *The Sentinel* said he "began to manifest a disposition of resistance expressing a determination not to be hanged." He asked to be shot instead and continued to struggle so much that the officers decided to keep the shackles on his wrists.

A few moments before 6:00 a.m., the time appointed for the execution, the prisoners were brought out to the scaffold accompanied by the Rev. Father McGuicken who had previously administered the Holy Eucharist to Barry and the rites of baptism to Palsk.

On the scaffold, Barry, while obviously weak from his illness, showed no sign of trepidation, but in the words of *The Sentinel* reporter, "sustained himself throughout the trying scene with the utmost fortitude and coolness." One cannot help wondering how much of his demeanor was due to fortitude and how much to simple resignation.

Again Palsk went to the other extreme. *The Sentinel* said he "behaved in a very excited manner and indulged in the most foul and blasphemous language, cursing the King George man [presumably the hangman] and his Indian accomplice, endeavoring all the while to extricate himself from his pinions."

A journalist for an American newspaper has him shouting out, "Don't tie me! Don't tie me! I am not woman!" as he was readied for the noose. "I kill ten white men. It was good. I should kill many more."

When one of the officers produced a hood and tried to place it over Palsk's head, he wrenched himself away.

"Put it on King George man [Barry] Do it all to King George man first." They managed to secure him finally and in that moment of comparative calm the executioner drew the bolt and the drop fell with a dull thud, sending both prisoners spinning and kicking into eternity.

After the bodies had hung for half an hour, *The Sentinel* said Dr. Bell examined them. He pronounced both men dead. They were cut down immediately and "conveyed in coffins to the place of interment near the burial ground at Richfield. By seven o'clock the scaffold was removed and nothing remained to show that any unusual event had occurred."

The report said that while neither man had made a public confession, Barry must have confessed to the priest in order to receive absolution.

"If he did so, the tenor of it will never be communicated to human ears as the laws of the Romish church forbid the revealing of secrets made at the confessional."

For the residents of Barkerville, once the hangings were behind them, life went back to its usual paths. In time a rumor would spring up that the men had been hanged from a cottonwood tree near the courthouse, and wags would tell the credulous that the remains of the rope could be seen swinging from "The Hanging Tree" for many years afterwards. Alas, the tree didn't have a branch strong enough from which to hang anyone.

Judge Begbie would be called "The Hanging Judge," but only after his death. History shows that, in spite of his fiery nature, he had no great love for sentencing people to death and did not deserve the epithet.

Nine years after he examined the executed men as they hung from the scaffold, Dr. Bell would himself be dead at the age of 53.

Del Moses lived on in Barkerville, continuing his careful journal entries, shaving chins, clipping hair and selling odds and ends from his back room until his death in 1890. His death certificate, signed by Dr. Hugh Watt, listed him as being seventy-four years of age, a Protestant, and still a barber by occupation. His birthplace was listed as England and the cause of death on January 3, 1890, was given as "inflammation of the bladder." After this come the words "10 days." Perhaps this is a reference to the duration of his illness. The death was registered on January 4.

So there it is. Charlie had been murdered and his murderer hanged. Both were in their graves — Charlie's preserved as a provincial historic site and Barry's unmarked and lost among numerous others on the hillsides overlooking Williams Creek.

End of story? Not really. What is told about Charlie in these pages is just about all that is known, but there is so much more to discover. We remember him, but we still know very little about him. Were it not for the ugly manner of his death, he would have been lost forever among scores of other young men who died seeking gold in the Cariboo. So the search for the real Charles Morgan Blessing goes on…

• • •

1. Taken directly from the records. In that era siwash house referred to a hut or Indian house.

The Prospector's Ten Commandments

While much of the credit for the comparatively peaceful nature of the Cariboo goldfield communities has gone to Judge Matthew Baillie Begbie and the police force, there is more to it than that.

Much recognition must go to the miners themselves; oddballs and eccentrics abounded, but in many ways the peacefulness was due simply to decent men behaving decently. The miners even had their own version of The Ten Commandments:

1) Thou shalt have no other claim but one.

2) Thou shalt not make for thyself any false claim, nor take on the likeness of a mean man by jumping one.

3) Thou shalt not go prospecting before thy claim gives out; neither shalt thou take thy money or gold dust to the gaming table.

4) Thou shalt remember what thy friends do at home on the Sabbath. Six days thou mayest dig or pick all the body can stand, but on Sunday thou shalt wash all thy dirty shirts and darn all thy stockings.

5) Think more of the gold and how to make it fastest than how thou wilt enjoy it.

6) Thou shalt not kill thine own body by working in the rain.

7) Thou shalt not grow discouraged and think of going home before thou hast made thy "pile."

8) Thou shalt not pick out specimens from the company pan and put them in thy mouth or purse.

9) Thou shalt not tell false tales about any "gold diggers."

10) Thou shalt not covet thy neighbour's gold or his claim: neither shalt thou undermine his bank in following a lead, move his stake, or wash tailings from his sluice.

Index

Sullivan, John Howe (special constable) 23, 24, 64, 65, 66, 67, 68, 72, 73, 82

T

13 Mile House 24, 68, 69, 70, 75, 81, 90
Thompson, Mr. H. 71, 72, 86
Tranquille Creek 12
Travailot, O.G. 38
true bills 78
Twelve-Foot Davis (*see* Davis, Henry Fuller)

V

Van Winkle 6, 15, 19, 20, 51, 54, 64, 69, 70, 81, 82, 90
~ Creek 15
Vancouver Island 12, 16
Victoria 16, 17, 64
Fort 12
Viscount Milton 27

W

wages 32, 40
Walkem, Mr. G.A. (defense counsel for Palsk) 87, 88, 89
Walker, Mr. H.P. (prosecutor) 78, 87
Wallace, Alexander 75, 76
Wallace, George 77
Wallace's 13 Mile House (*see* 13 Mile House)
Washburn, Mr. 71, 84
Washington, Territory of 11
Watt, Hugh (doctor) 95
Wells (town) 8, 32
Wilcox, Mr. S.J. 71, 72, 82, 84

Williams Creek 6, 7, 15, 17, 19, 20, 22–25, 33, 35, 47, 41, 47 (photo), 56, 57, 63, 64, 65, 66, 68, 69, 72, 76, 81, 86, 91, 95

Y

Yale 13, 14 (photo), 15, 17, 23, 24, 26, 41, 51, 64, 65, 67, 68, 82, 86
Yukon 31

More HANCOCK HOUSE history & biography titles

Afloat in Time
Jim Sirois
ISBN 0-88839-455-1
5.5 x 8.5 • sc • 288 pages

**Alaska in the Wake
of the North Star**
Loel Shuler
ISBN 0-88839-587-6
5.5 x 8.5 • sc • 224 pages

Beyond the Northern Lights
W. H. Bell
ISBN 0-88839-432-2
5.5 x 8.5 • sc • 288 pages

Bootlegger's Lady
Edward Sager
ISBN 0-88839-976-6
5.5 x 8.5 • sc • 286 pages

Broken Arrow #1
John M. Clearwater
ISBN 978-0-88839-596-2
5.5 x 8.5 • sc • 160 pages

**Captain McNeill and His
Wife the Nishga Chief**
Robin Percival Smith
ISBN 0-88839-472-1
5.5 x 8.5 • sc • 256 pages

Cold Lead
Mark Dugan
ISBN 0-88839-559-0
5.5 x 8.5 • sc • 176 pages

Crazy Cooks & Gold Miners
Joyce Yardley
ISBN 0-88839-294-X
5.5 x 8.5 • sc • 224 pages

Curse of Gold
Elizabeth Hawkins, Jack Mould
ISBN 0-88839-281-8
5.5 x 8.5 • sc • 288 pages

Deadman's Clothes
Dale Davidson
ISBN 0-88839-608-2
5.5 x 8.5 • sc • 144 pages

Descent Into Madness
Vern Frolick
ISBN 0-88839-321-0
5.5 x 8.5 • sc • 361 pages

Discovery at Prudhoe Bay: Oil
John M. Sweet
ISBN 978-0-88839-630-3
5.5 x 8.5 • sc • 304 pages

A Doctor's Notes
T.F. Godwin, MD, FRCP(C)
ISBN 978-088839-654-9
5.5 x 8.5 • sc • 368 pages

Fogswamp
Trudy Turner, Ruth McVeigh
ISBN 0-88839-104-8
5.5 x 8.5 • sc • 255 pages

Fraser Canyon
Lorraine Harris
ISBN 978-0-88839-182-7
5.5 x 8.5 • sc • 64 pages

**Frontier Forts & Posts of the
Hudson's Bay Company**
Kenneth E. Perry
ISBN 0-88839-598-1
8.5 x 11 • sc • 96 pages

**Gold Creeks and
Ghost Towns (BC)**
N. L. Barlee
ISBN 0-88839-988-X
8.5 x 11 • sc • 192 pages

**Gold Creeks and
Ghost Towns (WA)**
N. L. Barlee
ISBN 0-88839-452-7
8.5 x 11 • sc • 224 pages

Good Lawyer Bad Lawyer
David Nuttall
ISBN 0-88839-315-6
5.5 x 8.5 • sc • 256 pages

Incredible Gang Ranch
Dale Alsager
ISBN 0-88839-211-7
5.5 x 8.5 • sc • 448 pages

Into the Savage Land
Ernest Sipes
ISBN 0-88839-562-0
5.5 x 8.5 • sc • 160 pages

Jailbirds & Stool Pigeons
Norman Davis
ISBN 0-88839-431-4
5.5 x 8.5 • sc • 144 pages

Journal of a Country Lawyer
E. C. Burton
ISBN 0-88839-364-4
5.5 x 8.5 • sc • 240 pages

Klondike Paradise
C.R. Porter
ISBN 0-88839-402-0
8.5 x 11 • sc • 176 pages

Lady Rancher
Gertrude Minor Roger
ISBN 0-88839-099-8
5.5 x 8.5 • sc • 184 pages

**Lewis & Clark Across
the Northwest**
Cheryll Halsey
ISBN 0-88839-560-4
5.5 x 8.5 • sc • 112 pages

Loggers of the BC Coast
Hans Knapp
ISBN 0-88839-588-4
5.5 x 8.5 • sc • 200 pages

**Mattie: Wyatt Earp's
Secret Second Wife**
E.C. (Ted) Meyers
ISBN 978-088839-628-0
5.5 x 8.5 • sc • 288 pages

Nahanni Trailhead
Joanne Ronan Moore
ISBN 0-88839-464-0
5.5 x 8.5 • sc • 256 pages

**New Exploration of the
Canadian Arctic**
Ronald E. Seavoy
ISBN 0-88839-522-1
5.5 x 8.5 • sc • 192 pages

Out of the Rain
Paul Jones
ISBN 0-88839-541-8
5.5 x 8.5 • sc • 272 pages

Outposts & Bushplanes
Bruce Lamb
ISBN 0-88839-556-6
5.5 x 8.5 • sc • 208 pages

Puffin Cove
Neil Carey
ISBN 0-88839-216-8
5.5 x 8.5 • sc • 178 pages

Raven and the Mountaineer
Monty Alford
ISBN 0-88839-542-6
5.5 x 8.5 • sc • 152 pages

Rivers of Gold
Gwen & Don Lee
ISBN 0-88839-555-8
5.5 x 8.5 • sc • 204 pages

Ruffles on my Longjohns
Isabel Edwards
ISBN 0-88839-102-1
5.5 x 8.5 • sc • 297 pages

More HANCOCK HOUSE history & biography titles

Shaking the Feather Boa
E. C. (Ted) Burton
ISBN 978-088839-609-9
5.5 x 8.5 • sc • 192 pages

**Songs of the
Pacific Northwest**
Philip J. Thomas
ISBN 978-0-88839-610-5
8.5 x 11 • sc • 208 pages

**Stagecoaches Across the
American West 1850-1920**
John A. Sells
ISBN 978-0-88839-605-1
8.5 x 11 • sc • 336 pages

Timeless Trails of the Yukon
Dolores Cline Brown
ISBN 0-88839-584-5
5.5 x 8.5 • sc • 184 pages

**Time Travel in
North Vancouver**
Sharon J. Proctor
ISBN 978-0-88839-629-7
8.5 x 11 • sc • 112 pages

Tomekichi Homma
K.T. Homma, C.G. Isaksson
ISBN 978-0-88839-660-0
5.5 x 8.5 • sc • 72 pages

Vancouver's Bravest
Alex Matches
ISBN 978-0-88839-615-0
8.5 x 11 • sc • 352 pages

**Walter Moberly and the
Northwest Passage by Rail**
Daphne Sleigh
ISBN 0-88839-510-8
5.5 x 8.5 • sc • 272 pages

**White Water Skippers
of the North**
Nancy Warren Ferrell
ISBN 978-0-88839-616-7
5.5 x 8.5 • sc • 216 pages

Wild Roses
dutchie Rutledge-Mathison
ISBN 0-88839-625-2
8.5 x 11 • hc • 72 pages

Wild Trails, Wild Tales
Bernard McKay
ISBN 0-88839-395-4
5.5 x 8.5 • sc • 176 pages

Wings Over the Wilderness
Blake W. Smith
ISBN 978-0-88839-595-7
8.5 x 11 • sc • 296 pages

Wild Canadian West
E. C. (Ted) Meyers
ISBN 0-88839-469-1
5.5 x 8.5 • sc • 208 pages

Yukon Gold
James/Susan Preyde
ISBN 0-88839-362-8
5.5 x 8.5 • sc • 96 pages

Yukon Riverboat Days
Joyce Yardley
ISBN 0-88839-386-5
5.5 x 8.5 • sc • 176 pages

Yukoners: True Tales
H. Gordon-Cooper
ISBN 0-88839-232-X
5.5 x 8.5 • sc • 144 pages

www.hancockhouse.com